Mindful Magic

A Guide to Modern Witchcraft for Mental Wellness & Self-Care

Kelsey Pearce

Contents

Preface

To the Parent

We understand that the idea of your teenager exploring modern witchcraft may raise some concerns. It's important to recognize that the form of witchcraft discussed in this book is not about dark magic or harmful practices. Instead, it's a spiritual and wellness approach that encourages mindfulness, self-reflection, and a deeper connection with nature.

Modern witchcraft can be a valuable tool for teenagers to manage stress, explore their identities, and cultivate a sense of empowerment. This book does not promote or denounce any specific religious beliefs and respects and complements all spiritual and religious backgrounds. We invite you to keep an open mind and see this as an opportunity for your teenager to learn about new perspectives on self-care.

While the examples are geared toward a teenage audience, there is nothing preventing any age group from benefiting from the content. Share with your teen and explore your own 'witchiness'.

Introduction

A New Perspective on Self-Care

Our society is moving at an ever-increasing rate. Integration and reliance on technology impact almost every minute of our day. In today's fast-paced world, self-care has become an essential part of maintaining mental health and well-being. As teenagers navigate the challenges of growing up in a complex world, exploring different self-care practices can help them find balance and peace. One such avenue that has gained popularity and may appeal to you is modern witchcraft.

Modern witchcraft offers an easily adaptable and inclusive counterbalance to the fast-paced and technology-centric day-to-day.

While a considerable portion of the book will be dedicated to ritual and spellcraft, its core concept is to help readers understand how becoming a practitioner can create a positive mental health environment.

Note: If you are in a mental health crisis or have mental health concerns, please contact the appropriate mental health expert or discuss with your family.

As a teenager, I was drawn to witchcraft. At the time, I lived in suburbia, where every house looked the same, and for the most part, so did my peers. I felt like I existed on the fringe of 'normal' society. With hindsight, most likely, it was a feeling shared by the majority. I found magic in exploring small shops in the city annexes. There was an aesthetic I enjoyed as well as a connection to a different community separate from my day-to-day boring. I also felt a sense of maturity and empowerment that helped me determine the sameness of my tribe.

Over the years, my relationship with magic and witchcraft has evolved. Sometimes, witchcraft will play a smaller role in my day; at other times, I seek it out like an old friend. I have come to understand that when I am most unsure or anxious, my magic reaches back out and continues to empower me.

Since the age they showed interest both my daughter and son have also had the opportunity to explore spells, crystals, meditation, cleansing rituals, anything they wanted as long as it was safe. As they enter their teenage years, I hope their magic reaches back out to them to provide them with the strength and sense of self to navigate into adulthood.

This chapter introduces the concept of modern witchcraft, clarifies common misconceptions, and discusses its potential benefits as a complementary practice to traditional Western medicine. You may be eager to jump into crystals or sigils, but take a moment to understand the larger context of witchcraft in history and how it can easily blend in with traditional lifestyles.

The Inclusivity of Modern Witchcraft

Modern witchcraft is a spiritual practice that transcends gender, race, sexual orientation, and cultural backgrounds, making it inherently inclusive. At its core, witchcraft is about connecting with the energies of the universe, exploring personal spirituality, and expressing one's unique identity. Unlike many traditional religious systems that may have rigid structures and dogmas, modern witchcraft celebrates diversity and individuality. This flexibility allows practitioners to tailor their practices to align with their personal beliefs, values, and experiences, fostering a welcoming environment for all.

The inclusivity of modern witchcraft is reflected in its open acceptance of various deities, spiritual entities, and forms of magic. Whether you resonate with gods and goddesses from different pantheons, nature spirits, or simply the energy of the elements, there is space for you within this practice.

The community encourages self-exploration and expression, allowing each individual to define their path without judgment or restriction.

In addition, modern witchcraft often emphasizes social justice, equality, and the celebration of marginalized voices. Many practitioners use their spiritual practices to advocate for inclusivity, diversity, and environmental stewardship, making it a dynamic and evolving tradition that aligns with contemporary values. By embracing the rich tapestry of human experience, modern witchcraft creates a supportive and empowering space for everyone, allowing each person to find their unique way to connect with the magical and mystical aspects of life. Whether through solitary practice or within a community, the magic of modern witchcraft is open to all who seek it, regardless of how they identify or where they come from.

For this book, we will use the terms "practitioner," "witch," "spellcaster," or some combination. These terms honour the diversity of those who practice modern witchcraft without ascribing a specific gender identity. However, as an individual, embrace the terminology that resonates with you. There are many words that could be used to identify a practitioner of magic.

This book is not intended to convert anyone to a particular belief system but to offer tools and ideas that can enhance personal well-being.

It's important for both teens and parents to understand that modern witchcraft is a flexible and adaptable practice. It can be integrated with other spiritual or religious practices or standalone as a secular self-care practice. The focus is on personal empowerment, mindfulness, and a connection to the natural world.

As you explore the concepts and practices presented in this book, remember that they are inclusive and respectful of all beliefs. Whether you're seeking to deepen your existing spiritual practice or simply looking for new ways to manage stress and anxiety, modern witchcraft offers a versatile and supportive approach to self-care.

Cultural Appropriation

Cultural appropriation is a challenging concept. It is sometimes difficult to know if something we believe is mainstream may hold a specific spiritual meaning for another culture and be deemed offensive. A cultural belief may resonate with you but not be part of your culture and be perceived as appropriation.

For example, many modern practitioners might use smudging, a sacred Indigenous ritual that involves burning sage, in their rituals purely for aesthetic reasons or as a general tool for "cleansing negative energy." However, smudging is deeply rooted in the spiritual traditions of Indigenous peoples of North America and carries specific cultural and spiritual meanings. When non-Indigenous practitioners use sage without understanding or acknowledging these traditions or without obtaining the herb sustainably and respectfully, they can diminish the ritual's sacredness and contribute to the commodification (the act of treating something as a commodity) of a practice that is often sacred and culturally significant.

We have seen in sitcoms a friend or family member arriving at someone's home ready to cleanse the negative energy out of the room or home after a breakup. It may make so some laughs, but this form of cultural appropriation not only disrespects the original culture but can also perpetuate harm, especially when such practices are stripped of their context and commercialized. It's essential for modern witchcraft practitioners to be mindful, educated, and respectful when incorporating elements from other cultures.

I do not expect that in your personal practice, you will research the cultural significance of every aspect of your spellcraft. If you approach all of your magic intending to do no harm and be respectful, there should not be any harm. If you share your rituals with others, it would be appropriate to make sure you are not perpetuating any stereotypes or unknowingly being disrespectful. If you intend to make a profit from your magic, extra care should be taken to ensure it is done with respect.

It is okay that you may feel drawn to a particular aspect of magic despite not being part of your existing culture. These magical practices still exist because of their appeal and benefits. I am not from a Norse heritage but I feel a connection to runes. There is magic in the symbolism that suits me.

If your approach is ever challenged, be open to learning that person's perspective and be willing to acknowledge and apologize for any inadvertent disrespect. Be prepared to make a shift. The wonderful thing about spellcraft is the flexibility.

Definition of Modern Witchcraft and Its Historical Context

Modern witchcraft, also known as contemporary witchcraft or neo-paganism, is a spiritual practice that draws from various historical traditions, including Wicca, paganism, and folk magic. It emphasizes a connection to nature, personal empowerment, and using rituals and symbols to support personal growth and well-being. Unlike the sensationalized portrayals in movies and TV shows, modern witchcraft is a peaceful and introspective practice that encourages individuals to explore their inner selves and the world around them.

Across history, what we would refer to as witchcraft has been both revered and feared. In some cultures, a practitioner could hold a prominent place in a community or exist on the fringe of society. Today, witchcraft is often misunderstood and associated with negative stereotypes. However, its true roots are grounded in ancient practices that honoured the cycles of nature and sought to understand the mysteries of the universe. In modern times, witchcraft has evolved into a diverse and inclusive practice that focuses on self-discovery, healing, and community.

Clarifying Misconceptions: Pop Culture vs. Modern Witchcraft

Pop culture often depicts witchcraft as a fantastical or malevolent force, complete with spells, potions, and supernatural abilities. However, this portrayal is far from the reality of modern witchcraft. In truth, modern witchcraft is more akin to a spiritual and self-care practice than the dramatic depictions seen in media. It involves mindfulness, meditation, and rituals that help individuals connect with their inner selves and the natural world.

Modern witchcraft does not involve hexes or harmful magic. Instead, it focuses on positive intentions, personal growth, and fostering a deeper understanding of oneself and others. It's about creating sacred spaces, practicing gratitude, and using simple tools like crystals, herbs, and candles to enhance mindfulness and reflection.

But have no fear—despite not having all the flash and special effects of television or movies, creating your own rituals and spells can be quite fun and exhilarating.

Modern Witchcraft and Western Medicine: A Complementary Approach

It's important to note that modern witchcraft is not a replacement for traditional Western medicine. Instead, it can serve as a complementary practice that supports overall well-being. Just as one might use yoga or meditation to manage stress, modern witchcraft offers tools and practices that can enhance mental and emotional health. For example, mindfulness rituals, journaling, and nature walks can soothe and grounding activities that complement medical treatments or therapy.

Practicing modern witchcraft can also encourage teens to engage in self-care rituals that promote relaxation and reduce anxiety. For example, setting intentions during a new moon or practicing gratitude during a full moon can help teens feel more centred and connected to their goals. These practices are not meant to cure ailments, but to support a holistic approach to wellness.

Inclusivity and Respect for All Beliefs

In the following chapters, we will explore specific aspects of modern witchcraft, including rituals, tools, and the symbolism of natural elements. Each chapter will provide practical tips and activities that can enhance mental health and well-being. Keep an open mind as you read, and remember that this journey is about discovering what works best for you. Whether you choose to embrace these practices fully or simply experiment with a few ideas, the goal is to empower yourself and find a path to greater self-awareness and peace.

In addition, this book does not cover every cultural belief. You may discover other elements on your path that speak to you.

How the Book is Structures

Chapters one through five explore the concepts of witchcraft, like ethics, nature, and community. These are foundational chapters in your journey. Chapters six through eighteen cover a variety of elements of witchcraft, including topics like crystals, herbs, runes, tarot, sacred animals, and more. Woven into these chapters are some spell examples, but the majority of spell work begins in chapter nineteen. Chapter nineteen covers creating spells and casting spells. Chapter twenty contains a number of spells and charms including supplies and instructions. The last chapter reviews how you can incorporate magic into your daily routines.

Spell Work: A New Perspective on Self-Care

Ritual: Setting Intentions for Mental Wellness
  Supplies
  - A small candle or candle alternative

  - A piece of paper

  - A pen or marker

Instructions

- Find a quiet space and light the candle.

- Write down your intention for mental wellness (e.g., "I am calm and resilient").

- Focus on your intention as you fold the paper and place it near the candle but away from the burning area.

- Sit quietly for a few moments, visualizing your intention manifesting in your life.

- Blow out the candle, symbolizing the release of your intention into the universe.

Chapter 1

UNDERSTANDING MODERN WITCHCRAFT

I magine being able to tap into your inner power, connect deeply with the natural world, and find a sense of peace and purpose in your everyday life. That's the essence of modern witchcraft. Unlike the fantastical portrayals of witches casting spells or flying on broomsticks, modern witchcraft is a practical and introspective way of life. It's about understanding yourself, respecting the earth, and using simple tools and rituals to create positive changes.

The Role of Intention and Symbolism in Modern Witchcraft

At the heart of modern witchcraft is the concept of *intention*. An intention is like a goal or desire that you focus your mind and energy on, whether it's something small, like feeling more confident at school, or something big, like making a positive impact in the world. By setting clear intentions, you harness your inner power and direct it toward what you want to achieve. You find that almost every spell or ritual we explore will centre around intent.

In modern witchcraft, symbolism plays a crucial role in focusing intention and channeling energy. Symbols serve as visual or physical representations of deeper meanings and intentions, helping practitioners to align their thoughts and actions with their spiritual goals. Traditional symbols, like the pentacle, ankh, and triquetra, carry rich histories and are often used in rituals and spells to invoke specific energies or concepts. For instance, the pentacle, a five-pointed star within a circle, is commonly associated with protection, balance, and the five elements of earth, air, fire, water, and spirit. However, it is essential to understand that symbols themselves are neutral; their power and meaning come from the intention and context provided by the practitioner.

One of the empowering aspects of modern witchcraft is the freedom to choose or create symbols that resonate personally. Practitioners are not bound to traditional symbols and can use anything that holds significant meaning for them. For example, a person might choose a feather to symbolize freedom, a seashell for emotional healing, or a tree for grounding and growth. These symbols can be incorporated into spells, rituals, or everyday life, acting as reminders of one's intentions and goals. The act of creating personalized symbols or sigils—unique, often abstract designs crafted to represent specific desires or outcomes—allows practitioners to connect more deeply with their intentions. A sigil, infused with personal significance, becomes a potent tool for manifestation, helping to focus the mind and direct energy toward achieving the desired outcome. Sigils will be reviewed in greater detail in a later chapter.

Using symbols is not exclusive to witchcraft; it permeates everyday life, often unconsciously. For example, someone signing a note with a heart symbol conveys affection or love. This simple act of adding a heart transforms a mere signature into a message imbued with warmth and care. In this way, symbols function universally as a means of communication, transcending words to express complex emotions and intentions. Whether through a pentacle, a handmade sigil, or a common symbol like a heart, the essence lies in the intention behind the symbol. Practitioners can choose symbols that feel right for them, avoiding any that do not resonate with their personal beliefs or aesthetic preferences.

Ultimately, symbols in modern witchcraft are tools for personal expression and spiritual practice. They are flexible and adaptable, allowing each practitioner to craft a unique spiritual path. This adaptability also demystifies the notion that certain symbols are inherently "good" or "bad." Instead, the focus is on the meaning and intention behind the symbol. This approach encourages practitioners to explore their own relationships with symbols, fostering a deeper understanding of their inner world and the energies they wish to work with. Whether drawing on traditional symbols or creating new ones, the practice of using symbols in witchcraft is a powerful way to connect with the self, set intentions, and engage with the world.

Key Principles: Respect for Nature, Personal Empowerment, and Mindfulness

Modern witchcraft is grounded in three key principles: respect for nature, personal empowerment, and mindfulness.

Respect for Nature: Modern witchcraft teaches us to honour and respect the earth and all living things. This means being mindful of our actions and their impact on the environment, whether through eco-friendly practices or simply appreciating the beauty of nature. Connecting with the natural world can help us find a deeper sense of belonging and peace.

We are all a part of nature; therefore it is important to respect yourself and others. No spellcraft should involve self-harm or harming others. *If you are experiencing any thoughts of harm, please engage your local specialized services for support.*

Personal Empowerment: Modern witchcraft is all about empowering yourself to take control of your life. It's about recognizing your inner strength and potential and using that power to overcome challenges and achieve your goals. This empowerment comes from self-awareness, confidence, and the belief that you have the ability to make positive changes in your life. Empowerment is not a selfish practice. In fact, someone who feels empowered often feels the courage to act on behalf of others and serve as a conduit. Self-improvement does not come at the cost of taking from others. There is enough energy in the universe to support us all.

Mindfulness: Mindfulness is the practice of being present and fully engaged in the moment. It's about paying attention to your thoughts, feelings, and surroundings without judgment. In modern witchcraft, mindfulness helps you stay grounded and focused, allowing you to make thoughtful decisions and respond to life's ups and downs with clarity and calmness.

You may find that practicing mindfulness allows you to slow your pace and act with more intention. Most of our lives are spent going through the motions without engaging with our surroundings or the surrounding people. While we may not achieve a hundred percent mindfulness, even the focus for tiny amounts of time can be impactful.

Modern witchcraft is about empowering yourself, respecting nature, and using mindfulness to create positive change.

Ethics of Witchcraft

The ethics of modern witchcraft are an essential aspect to consider, especially for teenagers who are exploring this spiritual path. Unlike some religious systems with strict codes of conduct, witchcraft emphasizes personal responsibility and the intention behind actions. This flexibility can empower, but it also means that practitioners must contemplate the ethical implications of their practices. In modern witchcraft, ethics often revolve around principles like "harm none" and respect for free will. The idea is to use magic in ways that benefit yourself and others, without causing harm or manipulating others against their will.

One of the fundamental ethical guidelines in witchcraft is often summarized by the Wiccan Rede: "An ye harm none, do what ye will." This principle encourages practitioners to pursue their desires and intentions freely as long as their actions do not cause harm. It's a reminder that the energy you put out into the world can have consequences, and being mindful of these consequences is crucial. For example, if you're casting a spell to help with a personal goal, it's important to consider whether achieving that goal could negatively impact others. Being thoughtful and considerate in your practice helps ensure your actions are aligned with your values and ethics.

Looking deeper at intention:

Let's say you have a nasty classmate. This person is rude, and you are convinced they are trying to sabotage you in front of your teacher. You are going to conduct a ritual to help manage this issue. As a practitioner, you need to determine your intention for the ritual. Do you focus your intention:

- On this person getting caught sabotaging you?

- Perhaps on getting what they deserve?

- Having the strength to stay positive when faced with this person?

- On this person becoming a better human being and less likely to insult or sabotage?

Let us say you focus your intention on that person getting a taste of their own medicine. A few days later, they fall down the stairs at school, landing on their butt and surrounded by classmates laughing at them. I am not saying you caused them to fall, but your energy wanted something to happen. This could lead to feelings of guilt or even a false sense of superiority.

However, let us push our energy to being positive and confident with this person. Unlucky them, they still fall down the stairs. You did not cause it, and maybe the positive energy you have been building allows you to be the first person to help them and check that they are okay.

This might seem like a stupid, far-fetched, and kind of corny example, but it serves to demonstrate the extremes of intention.

Another important ethical consideration in witchcraft is respecting the free will of others. This means avoiding practices that manipulate or control others without their consent. For instance, while it might tempt to use magic to influence someone's feelings or decisions, doing so without their knowledge or consent can be seen as a violation of their autonomy. Instead, modern witchcraft encourages focusing on self-improvement, personal growth, and healing. This focus respects the boundaries of others and empowers practitioners to take responsibility for their own lives and actions.

Let's look at another cliche example: Love Spells

If modern movies have taught us anything, love spells fail. They can fail for a whole host of reasons: the person finds out and is angry or hurt, the practitioner doesn't see their true match because they are focused on the wrong person, or the spell is successful, but the practitioner realizes they don't really like that person, or the spell makes a person become obsessive... Whatever the reason, it fails because it is the wrong intention.

So, what would be an appropriate love spell? Something with an inward intent that does not manipulate others. Consider what that spell could be, and we will review an option in a later chapter.

It's also worth noting that the ethics of witchcraft extend to how we treat the environment and the natural world. Many modern witches feel a deep connection to nature and strive to live in harmony with it. This can mean being mindful of the materials used in rituals, practicing sustainability, and showing gratitude and respect for the earth's resources. Whether you're gathering herbs, working with crystals, or simply spending time in nature, being respectful and responsible in your interactions with the natural world is a key aspect of ethical practice.

Ultimately, the ethics of modern witchcraft are about making conscious choices that reflect your values and respect the well-being of others. As a teenager exploring this path, it's important to think about the energy you want to contribute to the world and how your actions align with your personal beliefs. By being mindful and intentional, you can practice witchcraft in a positive, respectful, and empowering way for yourself and those around you.

Embracing Your Path

As you explore modern witchcraft, remember that it's a highly personal journey. There are no strict rules or requirements—what matters most is finding what resonates with you. Whether you're drawn to rituals, symbols, meditation, or simply spending time in nature, the goal is to cultivate a deeper understanding of yourself and the world around you. Embrace the practices that make you feel empowered and connected, and don't be afraid to create your own unique path.

Modern witchcraft is a journey of self-discovery, respect for nature, and personal growth. It's a way to bring positive energy into your life and navigate the challenges of being a teenager with grace and confidence. As you delve deeper into this practice, you'll find that it's not just about magic—it's about becoming the best version of yourself.

Spell Work: A New Perspective on Self-Care

Ritual: Brushing Your Teeth With Intention

Before you begin this ritual, set a clear intention. This can vary depending on what you would like to focus on. For example, if you are working on removing negativity from your thoughts or communication, you could say, "I purify my thoughts and words," or "I cleanse away negativity and prepare to speak with clarity." However, if you would like to work on speaking confidently or using your voice for a specific message, you might try "I cleanse away confusion and invoke confidence and determination."

Supplies

- Toothbrush

- Toothpaste or alternative

Instructions:
- As you brush, focus on the act of cleansing and purifying. Imagine that with each motion, you are sweeping away any negativity, miscommunications, or doubts from your mind and mouth.

- Visualize your mouth filling with light, symbolizing truth, honesty, and clarity in communication.

- After you have completed brushing, repeat an affirmation like, "My words are clear, true, and kind" or "I speak with confidence and integrity." This reinforces the magical intent and helps align your energy with your goals.

Chapter 2

HARNESSING THE MAGIC OF RITUALS AND ROUTINES

R ituals and routines, while often used interchangeably, serve distinct roles in our lives and hold unique meanings. A **ritual** is a set of actions performed in a specific order, often imbued with symbolic meaning and intention. It can be a daily practice, like lighting a candle and setting an intention each morning, or something reserved for special occasions, like celebrating a seasonal holiday. Rituals often carry a sense of purpose and mindfulness, allowing individuals to connect with deeper aspects of themselves or a greater spiritual presence. They are usually conducted with a specific outcome in mind, such as seeking clarity, expressing gratitude, or celebrating a milestone.

On the other hand, a **routine** is a series of habitual actions that we perform regularly, usually with little thought. Routines are the building blocks of our daily life, providing structure and predictability. They include everyday activities like brushing our teeth, commuting to school, or making coffee in the morning. While routines can become so ingrained that we perform them automatically, they are essential for maintaining order and efficiency in our lives. They help us manage time, reduce decision fatigue, and create a stable environment.

The primary difference between rituals and routines lies in their intent and consciousness. Rituals are imbued with intentionality and often involve a conscious awareness of the actions being performed, serving as a bridge between the mundane and the meaningful. They can transform ordinary moments into sacred experiences. Routines, however, are more practical and functional, focused on maintaining order and efficiency rather than fostering a sense of deeper connection. While both rituals and routines play crucial roles in daily life, rituals elevate the every day by infusing it with purpose and significance, whereas routines provide the framework for navigating the practical aspects of living.

In your non-magical life, what are some of your routines? Perhaps you brush your teeth after waking up in the morning. That would be a routine. Even taking the same route to school or a friend's home is a routine. Not a lot of thought is needed to carry out the routine. That isn't to say that something routine could not become a ritual. As we reviewed in the previous chapter, magic is about intent. Perhaps while you brush your teeth, you keep eye contact with yourself in the mirror and mentally repeat the affirmation, "I will have a positive, productive day." Now, brushing your teeth is a ritual.

Rituals and routines are like secret weapons for your mind and soul. When you do something repeatedly, it becomes a habit, and habits shape who you are. By creating positive rituals, you train your brain to focus on the good things in life, even when times get tough. It's like having a magic wand that you can use to cast a spell of calm and confidence in yourself whenever you need it.

One of the best things about rituals is that they don't have to be complicated or time-consuming. You can start small with simple actions that make you feel grounded and centred. For example, you might take a few deep breaths every morning when you wake up or say a positive affirmation to yourself in the mirror. These tiny moments of mindfulness can make a big difference in how you feel throughout the day.

Another way to use rituals is to create a special space for yourself, like a personal altar or a cozy corner in your room. This is a place where you can go to relax, reflect, and recharge your magical batteries. You can decorate your space with things that make you happy, like crystals or pictures of your favourite places in nature. When you spend time in your sacred space, you're sending a message to your mind and body that it's okay to let go of stress and worry.

The great thing about rituals and routines is that they're totally customizable. What works for one witch might not work for another, and that's okay! The key is to experiment and find the practices that resonate with you. Maybe you like to write in a journal every night before bed, or perhaps you prefer to do a quick yoga flow in the morning. The more you tune in to your own needs and preferences, the more powerful your rituals will become.

Of course, it's important to remember that rituals and routines aren't a substitute for caring for your physical and mental health. If you're struggling with serious stress or anxiety, it's always a good idea to talk to a trusted adult or a healthcare professional. But for everyday trials, having a few magical tools in your self-care toolkit can make a world of difference.

So, how can you incorporate rituals and routines into your life? One effortless way is to pick one or two things you want to do daily and make them purposeful. Maybe you have a crystal that resonates with you. Leave it on your nightside table, and every morning, touch it and be thankful for a new day. In the evening, you can repeat the action, expressing one thing you are grateful for that day, mentally imbuing the crystal with thankful energy, something you can use in a charm or talisman later.

Another tip is to get creative with your routines. Don't be afraid to put your own magical spin on things! Maybe you prepare tea a special way every time you do your homework or wear a certain crystal when you need an extra boost of confidence. The possibilities are endless; the more you personalize your rituals, the more meaningful they'll feel.

As you incorporate rituals and routines into your daily life, you might be surprised at how much more grounded and centred you feel. It's like having a secret superpower that you can tap into whenever you need it. And what's great about this is that you don't need any fancy tools or expensive ingredients to make magic happen. All you need is a little bit of intention, a dash of creativity, and a willingness to show up for yourself daily.

So go ahead and give it a try. Start small, be consistent, and trust in the power of your own magic. You can improve your life from the inside out with a few simple rituals and routines. And who knows? You might just discover that you're capable of more than you ever imagined.

The Caveat to Rituals:

What happens if you cannot complete your daily ritual or lose that talisman or special crystal?

After repeated ritualized steps, it may feel like the ritual itself is the magic, but it is not. You are the magic and your intention. If a ritual is missed, it will not be the end of the world, because the energy is still within you. Repeatedly forgetting a ritual or losing an artifact could be the universe letting you know you don't need to rely on that right now. This might be a perfect time to reflect on what or how you want to direct your intention. You are the practitioner and can rewrite the process.

Key Takeaway

Rituals and routines are powerful tools for managing stress, finding inner peace, and connecting with your magical self. By incorporating simple practices into your daily life, you can train your brain to focus on the positive and create a sense of calm and confidence that carries you through even the toughest times.

Spell Work: A New Perspective on Self-Care

Ritual: Morning Grounding Routine

Supplies:
- A small bowl

- Salt

- A glass of water

- Amethyst or crystal of choice

Instructions:
- Begin each morning by placing the amethyst in your dominant hand.

- Stand with your feet firmly on the ground, take a few deep breaths, and visualize roots growing from your feet into the earth.

- Dip your fingers in the salt and then in the water, symbolizing cleansing and grounding.

- Say a simple grounding affirmation (e.g., "I am grounded and ready for the day").

- Place the amethyst in your pocket or bag as a reminder of your ritual.

Chapter 3

CONNECTING WITH NATURE

In our fast-paced, modern world, it's easy to feel disconnected from the natural environment surrounding us. As a young witch, you possess a unique opportunity to harness the healing power of nature to cultivate balance, peace, and inner strength. This chapter explores the therapeutic benefits of connecting with nature, the practice of mindfulness in natural settings, and the symbolic use of the elements—earth, water, fire, and air—in modern witchcraft.

The Healing Power of Nature

Nature has an innate ability to heal and restore. When we spend time in natural environments, whether it be a forest, park, or beach, we experience a reduction in stress and an improvement in our mood. This phenomenon is not just anecdotal; scientific research supports it. Studies have shown that exposure to green spaces can lower cortisol levels—the hormone associated with stress—and increase endorphins, the body's natural mood enhancers. Even brief encounters with nature, like a short walk or sitting under a tree, can significantly improve how we feel.

Mindfulness in Nature

One of the most powerful ways to connect with nature is through mindfulness. Mindfulness involves being present and fully engaged in the current moment without judgment. Practicing mindfulness in natural settings allows you to become more attuned to the sights, sounds, and sensations around you. You might notice the delicate dance of sunlight through the leaves, the whisper of the wind, or the cool touch of the earth beneath your feet. These simple yet profound experiences can foster a deep sense of peace and clarity.

Grounding Exercises: Grounding is a practice that involves physically connecting with the earth. You can do this by walking barefoot on grass or soil or by sitting or lying directly on the ground. Grounding helps balance your energy and reduce feelings of anxiety or stress. As you ground yourself, visualize roots extending from the soles of your feet into the earth, drawing up its stabilizing and nurturing energy.

Action Steps to Connect with Nature

Here are some practical ways to incorporate nature into your daily life:

Daily Nature Walks: Set aside time each day for a nature walk, even if it's just around your neighbourhood. Use this time to practice mindfulness and observe the natural world around you.

Create a Sacred Space: Find a quiet spot in your backyard or a nearby park to create a sacred space. This could include natural objects like stones, feathers, or leaves or simply a peaceful place for reflection.

Nature Journaling: Start a journal to document your observations, thoughts, and feelings about nature. Include sketches, poetry, or simple notes about what you notice daily.

Learn About Local Nature: educate yourself about the flora and fauna in your area. Consider going on a nature scavenger hunt, attending a guided hike, or visiting a nature centre.

Incorporate Nature into Witchcraft: Use natural elements like stones, crystals, or herbs in your spells and rituals. You can also create art inspired by nature as a form of magic and self-expression.

What if Nature isn't as Accessible?

In the introduction, we highlighted that witchcraft is inclusive, and that includes our living environment. If you are in a city or the concrete jungle, it might be harder to immerse yourself in nature. But cities offer a unique opportunity to appreciate the resiliency and perseverance of nature. Does grass or weeds grow between the pavement or sidewalk cracks? Can you find a bird's nest behind the grocery store sign or other industrious places? Did it rain, and was there a layer of dust off the cars on the street? Moments like these are opportunities to connect with the strength of nature and natural elements. The weed pushing up through the crack could resonate with your grit and determination or your intention to build that perseverance.

Even if there is an abundance of nature around you, taking time to find the strength and resiliency in nature can provide meaningful meditative moments.

Exercise: Either look directly at or envision a blade of grass or weed growing up between cracks in concrete. Imagine the strength of that blade of grass to push up into the harsh environment. Imagine the roots. Do they go down deep, seeking nourishment? Are they a complex path of shallow roots holding on to the unforgiving concrete? How are you like that blade of grass? What about it would you want for yourself? How could you build that intention?

The Elements in Modern Witchcraft

In modern witchcraft, the elements—earth, water, fire, and air—are foundational symbols representing different aspects of life and personality. Connecting with these elements in nature and through various practices can provide insights into yourself and the world around you. For you exploring spellcraft, these elements offer a safe and meaningful way to engage with the natural world and develop personal rituals. Here's a deeper look at each element and simple items and practices that can represent and connect you to these powerful forces.

Earth

Represents: Stability, grounding, and physical nourishment.

Magical Direction: North

Ways to Connect: Earth is the element of solidity and stability, representing the physical world and our material existence. To connect with earth, you can spend time in natural environments such as forests, mountains, or gardens. Practicing grounding techniques, like walking barefoot on grass or soil, can help you feel more centred and connected to the planet. Tending houseplants or planting seeds can also connect to the earth element.

Examples of Items: Stones, crystals, salt, soil, and plants. For spellcraft, you might keep a small jar of soil from a meaningful place, a favourite crystal like amethyst or quartz, or a potted plant to symbolize growth and stability.

Water

Represents: Emotion, intuition, healing.

Magical Direction: West

Ways to Connect: Water is the element of fluidity and change, symbolizing our emotional and intuitive nature. Connecting with water can be as simple as visiting a nearby river, lake, or ocean or even taking a mindful bath. Reflecting on water's adaptability can remind you of your own emotional resilience and capacity for healing.

Examples of Items: Seashells, water from a natural source, a small bowl of water, or a seashell. For spellcraft, you might collect rainwater for use in rituals, use seashells to represent the ocean's energy, or keep a small bowl of water on your altar to symbolize calm and reflection.

Fire

Represents: Transformation, passion, energy.

Magical Direction: South

Ways to Connect: Fire is the element of transformation and passion, representing the spark of life and creativity. Engaging with fire can be done safely by lighting a candle, sitting by a campfire, or even watching the stars. The warmth and light of fire can inspire courage and creative expression.

Examples of Items: A piece of charcoal, a representation of the sun, an artificial candle, or a real candle if lit practicing fire safety. For spellcraft, lighting a candle with intention can be a powerful ritual, whether for setting goals, releasing negative energy, or invoking inspiration. Always practice fire safety and never leave candles unattended—the light from a fake candle can be just as effective.

Air

Represents: Intellect, communication, freedom.

Magical Direction: East

Ways to Connect: Air is the element of intellect and communication, symbolizing clarity and the breath of life. Connecting with air can involve observing the wind, watching birds, or practicing deep breathing exercises. Air encourages new ideas, open communication, and a sense of freedom.

Examples of Items: Feathers, an empty glass, a fan, or a wind chime/bell. For spellcraft, you might use a feather to represent the air element or ring a bell to clear the air and invite positive energies. Note: some practitioners may burn incense, and there are concerns about carcinogenic ingredients entering the respiratory systems. If you choose to use incense, ensure it is in a well-ventilated area or outdoors.

Spirit

Represents: The unifying force that connects all things, representing the divine or universal consciousness.

Magical Direction: No specification direction, but generally considered centre, upward, or inward all connecting to the greater universal energy.

Examples of Items: personal items of yourself or loved one, any magical element intended to represent spirit.

Integrating Elements into Spellcraft

Incorporating these elements into your spellcraft can be a simple yet profound practice. For example, you can create an altar with items representing each element, such as a plant for earth, a seashell for water, a candle for fire, and a feather for air. Focus on each element's qualities during meditation or ritual, drawing inspiration and guidance. You might also create small rituals to honour each element, like planting seeds (earth), collecting rainwater (water), lighting a candle (fire), or setting intentions with deep breaths (air).

Calling on the Elements Before Spellcasting

Each element represents different aspects of life and the natural world, and by calling on them before casting a spell, you can create a balanced and powerful energy field that enhances your magical work. It is not required to call on the elements for every spell, but the more complex spells may benefit from the additional ritual. It is also possible to call on specific element that compliments the spell being cast.

Face the Direction of Each Element

Earth: Face North, the direction associated with Earth. You can hold a stone, crystal, or a small dish of soil as a symbol of this element.

Air: Face East, the direction associated with Air. You might hold a feather or simply feel the air around you.

Fire: Face South, the direction associated with Fire. Light a candle or hold a matchstick as a representation of this element.

Water: Face West, the direction associated with Water. Hold a small bowl of water or a seashell as a symbol of this element.

Spirit: Finally, stand in the center of your space, recognizing that Spirit is present in all directions and within you.

Invoke the Elements

Earth: "I call upon the power of Earth. Bring your strength, stability, and grounding to my work. May your energy support and sustain this spell."

Air: "I call upon the power of Air. Bring your clarity, creativity, and communication to my work. May your energy guide and inspire this spell."

Fire: "I call upon the power of Fire. Bring your passion, transformation, and courage to my work. May your energy fuel and empower this spell."

Water: "I call upon the power of Water. Bring your intuition, healing, and flow to my work. May your energy cleanse and nourish this spell."

Spirit: "I call upon the power of Spirit. Unite all elements and connect me to the divine. May your energy harmonize and bless this spell."

Visualize

As you call upon each element, close your eyes and visualize the energy of that element surrounding you. See the Earth rising up to ground you, the Air swirling around to inspire you, the Fire igniting to empower you, the Water flowing to cleanse you, and the Spirit weaving it all together.

Acknowledge the Elements

After invoking each element, take a moment to feel its presence. Acknowledge its energy and express gratitude for its assistance in your work.

Begin Your Spell:

With the elements called upon and their energies aligned with your intention, proceed with your spell. Whether you're casting a circle, setting intentions, or performing a ritual, the elements will now be present to support and strengthen your magic.

Closing the Ritual

Once your spell is complete, it's important to release the elements, thanking them for their presence and assistance:

Earth: "Thank you, Earth, for your grounding and stability. I release you with gratitude."

Air: "Thank you, Air, for your clarity and inspiration. I release you with gratitude."

Fire: "Thank you, Fire, for your passion and transformation. I release you with gratitude."

Water: "Thank you, Water, for your healing and intuition. I release you with gratitude."

Spirit: "Thank you, Spirit, for your unity and divine connection. I release you with gratitude."

Visualize the energies returning to their natural state, leaving you grounded, centered, and at peace.

Safety and Mindfulness

As you explore these practices, always prioritize safety, especially when working with fire. Remember, the essence of spell craft lies in intention and respect for the natural world. Whether you're grounding yourself with earth, flowing with water's emotions, igniting fire's passion, or embracing air's freedom, the elements offer a rich tapestry of energies to explore and honour.

Key Takeaway

Connecting with nature is a continuous journey, not a destination. By consistently making efforts to embrace the natural world, you'll find that your inner landscape transforms in powerful ways. You'll feel more grounded, resilient, and in tune with the rhythms of the earth and your own soul. Remember, nature is not just a backdrop but a vital part of your magical and spiritual growth. Embrace its magic, and let it guide you to inner peace and strength.

Chapter 4

MINDFULNESS AND MEDITATION

I magine a quiet space, a moment just for you, where the chaos of the world fades away. This is the power of mindfulness and meditation—a gateway to inner peace and strength that you can access anytime, anywhere. As a new witch, you can integrate these practices into your daily life, creating a tapestry of resilience and self-care.

Meditation is a simple yet profound practice used for centuries to calm the mind and soothe the soul. It doesn't require any special equipment or mystical abilities—just a quiet spot and a few moments of your time. As you settle into a comfortable position, close your eyes, and breathe deeply, you can feel the stresses of the day melt away. This is the essence of meditation: a practice of stillness and awareness that brings clarity and calm.

Meditation in Modern Witchcraft

In modern witchcraft, meditation is crucial for tuning into your intuition, connecting with inner wisdom, and tapping into the natural energies around you. Whether you're casting a spell, setting an intention, or simply navigating life's challenges, meditation helps you stay focused, grounded, and true to yourself. It allows you to clear your mind, centre your energy, and align with your spiritual path.

Guided Meditations and Visualizations

One of the most effective ways to experience the benefits of meditation is through guided visualizations. These are meditative journeys that help you explore your inner world and connect with deeper aspects of yourself. Imagine closing your eyes and being transported to a serene forest with towering trees and a babbling brook. You can feel the soft moss underfoot, smell the earthy scent of the woods, and hear the gentle rustling of leaves.

In this peaceful place, you might encounter a wise old tree, its branches reaching out in a gesture of support. As you lean against its sturdy trunk, you feel a deep sense of connection and belonging. This visualization helps you tap into your inner strength and find a calm centre amidst life's chaos. Other guided meditations might involve surrounding yourself with a protective white light or visualizing your worries being carried away on a gentle breeze. The key is to find visualizations that resonate with you and make you feel empowered and at peace.

You can create your own meditative story and record it on your phone to play back to you, or there are other guided meditation applications on most forms of technology, often free. You can also have a clear intention and attempt to guide yourself to a destination with no oral prompting.

Mindfulness: A Daily Practice

Alongside meditation, mindfulness is a powerful practice for managing stress and enhancing well-being. Mindfulness involves being fully present in the moment and engaged in whatever you're doing without judgment or distraction. It's about noticing the little things—the warmth of the sun on your skin, the sweetness of a ripe strawberry, the sound of laughter—and savouring them with all your senses.

Practicing mindfulness can be as simple as taking a few deep breaths before a challenging task or pausing to appreciate the beauty of a sunset. It teaches you to be kind and gentle with yourself, even in difficult times. Mindfulness helps you break free from the cycle of worry and distraction, allowing you to experience life more fully and joyfully.

Combining Mindfulness with Witchcraft

When you combine mindfulness with the practices of witchcraft, you create a potent recipe for resilience and self-care. Mindfulness enhances your magical work by helping you focus your intentions and energies. It also cultivates a deeper awareness of the interconnectedness of all things, a fundamental principle in many spiritual traditions.

For instance, before casting a spell, you might take a moment to ground yourself, becoming fully present and centred. As you prepare your ritual, engage all your senses—notice the textures of the materials you use, the smells of the herbs, and the flicker of candle flames. This mindful approach deepens your connection to the magic you're working with and amplifies its effects.

Finding Inner Peace and Strength

Remember that you have the power to find peace, strength, and joy within you. Meditation and mindfulness are tools that help you access this inner wellspring, guiding you through life's challenges with grace and resilience. As you continue to explore these practices, you'll discover new ways to connect with your true self and the world around you.

By cultivating a regular practice of meditation and mindfulness, you not only enhance your mental and emotional well-being but also enrich your spiritual journey. Whether you're seeking to calm a busy mind, gain clarity on a hard decision, or simply find a moment of peace in a hectic day, these practices offer a reliable path to inner harmony.

So, take a deep breath, find a comfortable spot, and begin your journey inward. Embrace the quiet moments, the gentle breaths, and the simple joys of being present. In these moments, you will find the true magic of life—calm, clarity, and a profound connection to your inner world.

Practical Applications: Mindfulness and Meditation

One of the most accessible ways to practice modern witchcraft is through "mindfulness meditation". You don't need any special tools or skills to get started—just a quiet space and a willingness to focus. Here's a simple way to begin:

Find a Quiet Spot: Choose a comfortable place where you won't be disturbed. Sit or lie down in a relaxed position.

Focus on Your Breath: Close your eyes and take a few deep breaths. Focus on the sensation of the air entering and leaving your body.

Observe Your Thoughts: As you meditate, thoughts will naturally arise. Instead of getting caught up in them, simply observe them and let them pass, gently bringing your focus back to your breath.

Be Patient: Meditation takes practice. Start with a few minutes each day and increase the time as you become more comfortable.

Meditation helps calm the mind and allows you to tune into your inner self. With regular practice, you'll find it easier to stay present, manage stress, and feel more connected to your surroundings.

Chapter 5

BUILDING A SUPPORTIVE COMMUNITY

In the journey of exploring modern witchcraft and mindfulness, one of the most crucial aspects of mental well-being, especially for teenagers, is building a strong support network. This chapter focuses on the importance of community, how to find like-minded individuals, and the benefits of these connections. It also touches on respecting diversity and being mindful of online interactions.

The Solitary Witch

It's okay to be a solitary witch. Nothing in the witch's guide says you must be part of a larger community. However, if you have found yourself gravitating to modern witchcraft and feeling marginalized or unaccepted by your existing community, it may provide comfort to know that you are not alone. There are many other witches like you, and you are all connected with the same universal energy. It's comforting to know you are not alone, whether you choose to find other practitioners or remain on your own.

Guided Meditation: Connecting to Universal Energy and the Collective of Witches

This guided meditation helps you connect with the universal energy and collective consciousness of witches around the world. It aims to foster a sense of belonging, unity, and empowerment, easing any feelings of isolation or margin-alization.

Prepare: Find a quiet and comfortable space where you can sit or lie down without interruption. You may choose to hold a talisman or crystal to help focus your energy. However, it is unnecessary. Close your eyes, take a deep breath, and let yourself relax.

Grounding and Centering: Begin by taking a deep breath through your nose, allowing your lungs to fill completely. Hold your breath for a moment, then exhale slowly through your mouth. Repeat this process a few times, feeling the rise and fall of your chest and the gentle rhythm of your breath.

As you continue to breathe deeply, visualize roots extending from the base of your spine and the soles of your feet, reaching down into the earth. These roots connect you firmly to the ground, anchoring you to the nurturing and supportive energy of the Earth. Feel the stability and security of this connection, knowing that you are grounded and safe.

Drawing in Universal Energy: Imagine a soft, glowing light above your head. This light represents the infinite energy of the universe, a source of wisdom, love, and connection. As you breathe in, visualize this light slowly descending, entering the top of your head, and filling your entire being with warmth and illumination. This energy flows through you, clearing away any feelings of isolation, doubt, or negativity.

As the universal energy flows through you, feel it connect with the energy of the Earth, creating a harmonious balance within you. You are a conduit of this powerful, nurturing energy, both grounded and uplifted.

Connecting with the Collective of Witches: With the universal energy flowing through you, visualize yourself standing in a vast, open space. In all directions, countless points of light surround you. These lights represent the spirits of other witches, practitioners, and spiritual seekers worldwide.

Feel the energy and presence of these kindred spirits. Know that each light represents a person who, like you, seeks connection, understanding, and empowerment. As you focus on these lights, you may sense their diverse energies, each unique yet united in a shared purpose.

Sending and Receiving Energy: Imagine a gentle, golden thread of light extending from your heart, reaching out to connect with the surrounding lights. This thread represents love, compassion, and solidarity. As it touches each light, feel a sense of connection and unity growing stronger. You are not alone, but part of a vast, supportive community of witches and spiritual practitioners.

As these threads connect, you may also feel energy flowing back towards you. This energy carries the warmth of acceptance, the strength of shared experiences, and the wisdom of the collective. Let this energy fill you with a sense of belonging and purpose. You are part of a larger tapestry, woven together with others who walk a similar path.

Affirmation and Intention: Take a moment to set an intention or affirmation for yourself. You might say silently or aloud: "I am connected to the universal energy and the collective of witches. I am supported, loved, and never alone. My path is valid, and I walk it with confidence and grace."

Feel the truth of these words resonate within you. Let them strengthen your sense of self and your connection to the world around you.

Returning to the Present: Gradually, bring your awareness back to the present moment. Visualize the points of light and the golden threads gently fading, knowing that the connection remains even as you return to your everyday awareness.

Slowly wiggle your fingers and toes, feeling the solidity of the ground beneath you. Take a few deep breaths, and when you feel ready, gently open your eyes.

Conclusion: You are now back in your space, grounded and centred, carrying with you the warmth of the universal energy and the connection to your fellow witches. Remember that whenever you feel isolated or marginalized, you can return to this meditation and rekindle the sense of unity and support. You are never alone; you are a cherished part of a vibrant, magical community. Be thankful for this energy and know that other witches appreciate you being part of our collective energy.

The Importance of Community and Support Networks

If it suits your personality, being part of a supportive community can significantly enhance your experience with modern witchcraft and mental health practices. Just as a coven in traditional witchcraft provides a sense of belonging and shared purpose, your circle of support acts as a safe space where you can share your thoughts, learn from others, and find encouragement.

Imagine yourself in a serene garden, surrounded by friends who understand and uplift you. You're sipping herbal tea, exchanging stories, and absorbing the collective wisdom. This is the essence of a supportive community—a place where you feel seen, heard, and valued. The sense of belonging and connection you experience in such a group can be a powerful source of comfort and strength, helping you navigate the challenges of adolescence and beyond. But you do not need a garden, or tea, or even to meet in person. Connections can come in many ways.

Finding Your Tribe: Online and Offline

Identifying Your Interests: To find your tribe, start by reflecting on your interests and passions. Are you drawn to nature-based rituals, tarot reading, crystal healing, or perhaps astrology? These interests can be the starting point for finding like-minded individuals.

Local Connections: Look for local metaphysical shops, community centres, or libraries that host workshops and events on topics you're passionate about. Attending these gatherings can help you meet people who share your interests. For instance, a local crystal shop might host a crystal grid workshop or a community centre might offer yoga classes with a spiritual twist.

Online Communities: In today's digital age, social media and online platforms are invaluable tools for finding community. Websites, forums, Facebook groups, and Instagram pages dedicated to modern witchcraft, spirituality, and self-care are abundant. Join these groups and take part in discussions. Share your experiences, ask questions, and support others on their journey. However, while online communities can be incredibly supportive, it's essential to prioritize your safety and privacy. Be cautious about sharing personal information and be aware of the potential for misunderstandings or misrepresentations online.

If a group makes you uncomfortable or doesn't align with your values, leave the group. There are ample groups to join, or you can start your own.

Respecting Diversity and Finding Common Ground

Modern witchcraft is wonderfully inclusive, welcoming people from all backgrounds, cultures, and belief systems. As you connect with others, approach them with an open mind and a willingness to learn. Celebrate the diversity of perspectives and experiences, as this richness can deepen your understanding and appreciation of the world.

Focus on finding common ground. Shared values, such as a commitment to personal growth, a love for nature, or a dedication to self-care, can help build strong connections. When differences arise, view them as opportunities to learn and grow. Remember, there is no one "right" way to practice modern witchcraft, and being open to different approaches can enhance your own practice.

Nurturing Your Relationships

Once you've found your tribe, nurturing these relationships with care and intention is important. Here are some tips:

Regular Gatherings: Make time for regular meetups in person or virtually. These can be simple gatherings to discuss your spiritual practices, share new learnings, or perform rituals together.

Support and Encouragement: Be there for each other during tough times. Offer a listening ear, provide advice if asked, and celebrate each other's successes.

Open Communication: Maintain open and respectful communication. This helps in resolving conflicts and misunderstandings and keeps the group dynamic healthy.

Respect Boundaries: While it's important to be supportive, respect each other's boundaries and personal space. Everyone has different comfort levels with sharing and participation.

Growth and Evolution: Understand that relationships, like individuals, grow and change. As you and your friends evolve, your connections may shift. Embrace these changes and trust that they are part of the natural flow of life.

Cautions and Considerations

While building a community can enrich, it's important to be mindful of a few cautions:

Safety Online: Always prioritize your safety when engaging with online communities. Be cautious about sharing personal information, and be aware that not everyone may have good intentions.

Inclusivity and Respect: Be inclusive and respectful of all individuals, regardless of their backgrounds. Avoid cliques and exclusionary behaviour, which can harm the community's supportive nature. Expect the same behaviours from other members of the community. There may be a hierarchy within a particular community, but no one should be made to feel like they are of lesser value.

Avoiding Groupthink: While finding common ground is great, be wary of groupthink. Encourage individuality and critical thinking within your group. You are an individual and should celebrate that individuality.

Maintaining Balance: Ensure that your participation in these communities enhances your life rather than detracts from it. Balance online interactions with real-world experiences and personal time.

Key Takeaway

Building a circle of support through community and connections is a powerful aspect of modern witchcraft, particularly for a new witch navigating the complexities of life. It offers a space for growth, learning, and mutual support. By finding your tribe, respecting diversity, and nurturing these relationships, you can create a supportive environment that enhances your mental health and personal development. Remember, the right people will come into your life at the right time, bringing with them lessons and experiences that will enrich your journey. Even if you are a solitary witch, you are still part of a larger community.

Chapter 6

THE HEALING POWER OF HERBS, FLOWERS & ESSENTIAL OILS

D id you know that the natural world is full of magical tools you can use to feel calmer, happier, and more in control of your life? It's true! For centuries, witches have harnessed the power of herbs to soothe stress, boost their moods, and promote healing in body, mind, and spirit. The best part is you don't need a pointy hat or a bubbling cauldron to put this magic to work in your own life.

Safety and Precautions for the Use of Herbs, Flowers, and Essential Oils

As a new magic practitioner exploring the magical properties of herbs, flowers, and essential oils, it's essential to prioritize safety and take necessary precautions. These natural elements can enhance your spiritual practices but also require careful handling. This section provides key safety guidelines to ensure your magical journey is safe and enjoyable.

Understanding the Source:

When incorporating herbs, flowers, and essential oils into your practice, it's crucial to know the quality and origin of your products. Here are tips to ensure safety:

Food-Grade Products: If you consume herbs or flowers, whether as teas, in cooking, or in other edible forms, make sure they are food-grade. Not all herbs and flowers sold for magical or aromatic purposes are safe for ingestion. Look for products specifically labelled as food-grade and purchase them from reputable suppliers.

An uncomplicated way to do this is using grocery store teas and tisanes. These are safe to consume, barring any allergies.

Organic and Non-Toxic: If available, choose organic herbs and flowers. These are less likely to be contaminated with pesticides or other harmful chemicals. For essential oils, look for therapeutic-grade oils, which are typically pure and free from additives.

Proper Identification: Ensure that the herbs and flowers you use are correctly identified. Some plants can have toxic look-a-likes. If you're foraging or growing your own, invest in a reliable guide or consult with a knowledgeable source.

Foraging is a wonderful way to connect to the earth and be in nature. However, we need to be aware of not only the products we forage for but also of private property rules, sustainability, and handling foraged products...If this interests you, find a local foraging group or community event to ensure you are being respectful and safe.

Allergies and Sensitivities

Many herbs, flowers, and essential oils can cause allergic reactions or sensitivities. It's important to be mindful of your own and others' reactions to these substances:

Patch Test: Before using a new essential oil or herbal product on your skin, perform a patch test. Apply a small amount of the product (diluted in a carrier oil, if applicable) to a small area of your skin, such as your inner wrist or behind your ear. Wait 24 hours to see if any irritation or allergic reaction occurs.

Allergy Awareness: Be aware of common allergens, such as certain flowers like chamomile (related to ragweed) or essential oils like lavender. Always check for known allergies and consult with a healthcare provider if you have concerns.

Inhalation Caution: Certain herbs or essential oils, especially when diffused, may cause respiratory sensitivity in some individuals. If you have asthma or other respiratory conditions, use these products with caution and ensure good ventilation. Even something as yummy as cinnamon can have negative effects if breathed in.

Handling: Protect your skin and avoid cross-contamination with your kitchen herbs and spices. Wash and dry your hands and utensils thoroughly. Washing can be included in a mindful preparation or termination of a spell. Do not use anyone else's products without permission. The jar labelled basil may not always be basil.

Using Essential Oils Safely

Essential oils are highly concentrated extracts that require careful handling. Here are suggested safety tips:

Dilution with Carrier Oils: Never apply essential oils directly to your skin without diluting them in a carrier oil, such as jojoba, coconut, or olive oil. A typical dilution ratio is 1-2 drops of essential oil per teaspoon of carrier oil for topical use.

Photosensitivity: Some essential oils, especially citrus oils like lemon, lime, and bergamot, can increase your skin's sensitivity to sunlight, leading to burns or rashes. If you use these oils on your skin, avoid direct sun exposure for at least 12 hours.

Internal Use: Do not ingest essential oils unless under the guidance of a qualified healthcare professional. Even food-grade essential oils can be potent and potentially harmful if misused.

Keep essential oil use limited to a few drops in a diffuser or on a cotton ball.

Cleaning up Spills or Accidental Exposure of Essential Oils

Cleaning up essential oils requires careful attention, as they are highly concentrated and can be harmful if not managed properly. Avoid using water to clean up spills, as oil and water don't mix, and water can spread the oil rather than contain it. Instead, use an absorbent material like baking soda, flour, or kitty litter to soak up the oil. Once the oil is absorbed, carefully sweep up the material and dispose of it in a sealed plastic bag to prevent further exposure. For surfaces, wipe down the area with a cloth dampened with rubbing alcohol or a vinegar-water solution, as these can effectively break down the oil residue.

If essential oils come into contact with your skin or eyes, rinse the affected area thoroughly with a carrier oil, such as olive or coconut oil, rather than water, and then wash with soap and water. In case of ingestion or if there's any adverse reaction, seek professional medical help immediately. Essential oils are potent substances and can cause skin irritation, allergic reactions, or other health issues if misused. It's crucial to manage them with care and seek expert guidance when needed.

Handling Herbs and Flowers:

While herbs and flowers may seem harmless, they still require respectful and knowledgeable use.

Proper Dosage: Just like in cooking, dosage matters. Some herbs can have powerful effects, even in small quantities. Start with tiny amounts and gradually increase if needed, being mindful of their potency. Remember, using an herb or flower is symbolic; it does not require immense quantities.

Storage: Herbs and essential oils should be stored in a cool, dark place to maintain their potency and prevent spoilage. They should also be kept out of the reach of pets and children.

Avoiding Toxic Plants: Be cautious with plants that are toxic to humans and pets. Familiarize yourself with common poisonous plants, such as foxglove, belladonna, and some types of nightshade. Don't use them unless you are a hundred percent confident in their safety.

Responsible Use and Environmental Considerations:

Sustainable Sourcing: Choose sustainably sourced herbs and essential oils. Overharvesting can threaten plant species and ecosystems, and supporting ethical suppliers helps protect biodiversity.

Waste Disposal: Responsibly dispose of any used or expired herbs, flowers, or essential oils. Avoid pouring essential oils down the drain, as they can be harmful to aquatic life. Instead, absorb them with a natural material like cotton and dispose of them in the trash.

Incorporating herbs, flowers, and essential oils into your magical practice can be a deeply enriching experience. By following these safety and precautionary measures, you can enjoy their benefits while minimizing risks. Remember, the key to effective and safe magic is knowledge, respect for nature, and mindfulness of your own body and the world around you.

Alternatives to Using Herbs, Flowers, and Essential Oils

The last section wasn't meant to scare or deter; rather, it was designed to protect practitioners from inadvertently harming themselves or others. Using natural herbs, flowers, and essential oils is not the only way to incorporate these elements into your magic practice. Herbs and flowers can also be represented as symbolic in your spell. This is also a creative and sustainable alternative.

For example, you need lavender for a calming spell bag. You could write out the word lavender while visualizing the flower, thinking about its soothing aroma. Or you could draw or paint the flower. Herbs and flowers are well suited for watercolour paint, and watercolour paper is thicker, allowing it to be used in multiple spells.

While many faux plants look real, they are still artificial. While they can represent the plant you need for a spell, they are usually made with plastic or other materials that are not environmentally friendly. It is advised to avoid plastic plants.

Some practitioners may disagree about alternatives; remember that this is highly personal, and magic is well suited for creative alternatives when it aligns with intent. Not every person will have access to different herbs and flowers. Creating alternatives is a magical self-expression and shows how inclusive witchcraft can be.

Herbal & Flower Magic:

Herbs are more than just something that is sprinkled into spaghetti sauce and flowers are more than pretty decorations. There are magical properties to both herbs and flowers. Below are twenty herbs and flowers you may consider in your spellcrafting. Each includes how they can be used, descriptions, and some cautions. Also included is the plant's scientific name, which may provide additional depth if creating a visual representation of the plant.

Lavender (*Lavandula angustifolia*)

Attributes: Calming, soothing, promotes peace and relaxation.

Description: Lavender is a fragrant herb with purple flowers known for its calming properties. It can be used in sachets, teas, or as an essential oil to reduce stress and promote restful sleep.

Caution: Lavender can affect hormone levels and may have estrogenic effects. It is advisable for those with hormone-sensitive conditions (biological male or female) or pregnant women to consult a healthcare professional before use.

Rose (*Rosa spp.*)

Attributes: Love, beauty, compassion.

Description: Roses are classic symbols of love and beauty. Their petals can be used in baths, teas, or as offerings in love spells to enhance self-love and harmony.

Caution: Rose essential oil is generally safe, but avoid using it directly on the skin without dilution, as it can cause irritation. Be mindful that roses may contain pesticides, which should not be used in baths or consumable products.

Chamomile (*Matricaria chamomilla*)

Attributes: Relaxation, healing, protection.

Description: Chamomile is a gentle herb with small, daisy-like flowers. It is often used in teas for its calming effects and can be included in spells for relaxation and healing.

Caution: Chamomile may cause allergic reactions in individuals sensitive to ragweed or other related plants. It may interact with blood-thinning medications.

Sage (*Salvia officinalis*)

Attributes: Cleansing, purification, wisdom.

Description: Sage is a potent herb often used in smudging rituals to cleanse spaces of negative energy. Its leaves can also be used in cooking or as a tea to promote wisdom and clarity.

Caution: Sage should not be consumed in large quantities, as it contains thujone, which can be toxic in high doses. Pregnant or breastfeeding women should avoid excessive use.

Rosemary (*Salvia rosmarinus*)

Attributes: Memory, protection, love.

Description: Rosemary is a woody herb with needle-like leaves. It is used in cooking and as an incense in spells for memory enhancement, protection, and love.

Caution: Rosemary should be used cautiously by individuals with epilepsy, as it may provoke seizures. It is also not recommended in large amounts during pregnancy.

Basil (*Ocimum basilicum*)

Attributes: Prosperity, protection, love.

Description: Basil is a sweet, aromatic herb commonly used in cooking. It can also be used in spells to attract prosperity, protect, and enhance love energy.

Caution: While safe, basil essential oil should be used with caution and always diluted, as it can cause skin irritation.

Dandelion (*Taraxacum officinale*)

Attributes: Wishes, divination, resilience.

Description: Dandelions are common flowers with bright yellow blooms. They are often used in wish-making and divination, symbolizing resilience and the fulfilment of desires.

Caution: Dandelion may interact with diuretics and blood-thinning medications. Those with allergies to related plants (like ragweed) should exercise caution.

Thyme (*Thymus vulgaris*)

Attributes: Courage, strength, purification.

Description: Thyme is a small herb with fragrant leaves. It is used in spells of courage, strength, and purification. It can be burned as incense or used in cooking.

Caution: Thyme oil can irritate the skin and the mucous membranes. It should be diluted before topical use. Excessive consumption should be avoided during pregnancy.

Jasmine (*Jasminum spp.*)

Attributes: Love, spirituality, dreams.

Description: Jasmine is a fragrant flower known for its sweet scent. It is used in love spells, spiritual practices, and dream enhancement, often as an essential oil or tea.

Caution: Jasmine oil should not be ingested and must be diluted for topical use to prevent skin irritation. Pregnant women should avoid using jasmine in high doses.

Eucalyptus (*Eucalyptus spp.*)

Attributes: Healing, protection, purification.

Description: Eucalyptus is a tall tree with aromatic leaves. It is commonly used in healing and protection spells and can be diffused as an essential oil for purification.

Caution: Eucalyptus oil is toxic if ingested and can cause severe irritation when applied directly to the skin. It should be kept away from children and pets.

Marigold (*Tagetes spp.*)

Attributes: Protection, creativity, positivity.

Description: Marigolds are bright, cheerful flowers that symbolize positivity. They are used in protection spells and to encourage creativity. Marigold petals can be used in baths or as decorations.

Caution: Marigold can cause skin irritation in sensitive individuals. Its use should be avoided during pregnancy and breastfeeding.

Lemon Balm (*Melissa officinalis*)

Attributes: Happiness, calm, clarity.

Description: Lemon balm is a citrus-scented herb known for its calming effects. It is used in teas and spells to uplift the spirit, promote happiness, and provide mental clarity.

Caution: Lemon balm can interfere with thyroid medications and should be used with caution by individuals with thyroid disorders. It may also cause drowsiness.

Cinnamon (*Cinnamomum verum*)

Attributes: Prosperity, protection, passion.

Description: Cinnamon is a spice obtained from the bark of cinnamon trees. It is used in spells of prosperity, protection, and passion. It can be burned as incense or added to foods.

Caution: Cinnamon can cause skin irritation or allergic reactions if applied directly. Ingesting large quantities can cause liver damage due to coumarin content, especially in "cassia" cinnamon.

Yarrow (*Achillea millefolium*)

Attributes: Healing, courage, protection.

Description: Yarrow is a hardy herb with clusters of tiny flowers. It is used in healing and protection spells and can be made into teas or dried for other magical uses.

Caution: Yarrow may cause allergic reactions, particularly in individuals sensitive to ragweed. It can also interact with blood-thinning medications.

Violet (*Viola odorata*)

Attributes: Love, protection, tranquility.

Description: Violets are small, delicate flowers with a sweet fragrance. They are used in love and protection spells and to promote tranquility. Violets can be used in teas or as offerings.

Caution: Violet leaves are generally safe, but consuming large amounts can cause stomach discomfort. External use should be cautious if sensitive to the plant.

Mint (*Mentha spp.*)

Attributes: Clarity, communication, prosperity.

Description: Mint is a cooling herb with a fresh, clean scent. It is used in spells for mental clarity, enhancing communication, and attracting prosperity. It can be used fresh or dried.

Caution: Mints (peppermint, spearmint...) can exacerbate acid reflux symptoms. Use mint oils diluted to prevent skin irritation.

Calendula (*Calendula officinalis*)

Attributes: Healing, protection, joy.

Description: Calendula, also known as marigold, has bright orange or yellow flowers. It is used in healing spells, protection rituals, and to bring joy. Calendula petals can be used in baths or ointments.

Caution: Calendula may cause allergic reactions in people sensitive to the Asteraceae/Compositae family. Pregnant and breastfeeding women should avoid internal use.

Bay Leaf (*Laurus nobilis*)

Attributes: Protection, success, wishes.

Description: Bay leaves come from the bay laurel tree and are often used in cooking. They are also used in spells for protection, success, and wish-making, often written on and burned.

Caution: Bay leaves are not typically consumed whole because of their sharp edges, which can pose a choking hazard or cause digestive discomfort. Bay essential oil should be diluted for topical use.

Clove (*Syzygium aromaticum*)

Attributes: Protection, love, purification.

Description: Cloves are aromatic flower buds used as a spice. They are used in spells for protection, love, and purification. Cloves can be used whole, ground, or as an essential oil.

Caution: Clove oil is very potent and can cause burns or irritation if used undiluted. It should be used cautiously, especially by individuals with bleeding disorders, as it can affect blood clotting.

Each herb and flower has unique magical and therapeutic qualities, but it's essential to approach them with respect and caution. Always research thoroughly and consult with professionals if you are unsure about the safe use of any plant or essential oil.

Key Takeaways

Herbs, flowers, and essential oils may enhance your magic spellcrafting. You don't need fancy equipment or hard-to-find ingredients to incorporate herbs into your daily life. The importance is recognizing the intent and representation of the herbal infusion. Caution should always be taken when considering using actual plant material.

Chapter 7

CRYSTAL & MINERALS: HARNESSING EARTH'S ENERGY

C rystals are gorgeous, glittering gems that come from deep within the earth. Each type of crystal vibrates with its own unique energy, and by keeping a crystal close by, you can tap into its healing vibes to shift your mood and mindset in a more positive direction. Crystals and minerals also help focus a witch's intention or energy.

This chapter is not limited to just crystals as a magical element. This chapter will also review minerals, including salt, the crystal structure, and how it can be used in spells. There is also a section of sacred geometry (don't worry, it isn't math), as well as magical properties of crystal alternatives like sea glass and river rock.

While the properties of these elements are touched on, remember that your intuition and connection are just as important, if not more important. You don't need to possess every crystal type in all its formats. Hold a crystal in your hand and gaze at its colours, markings, or flaws. If that crystal resonates with you, it likely will have a purpose.

I have a piece of tumbled bright green serpentine stone that I placed on my end table. It is the only crystal to ever take that position; it just felt right. At the time, I hadn't even known serpentine's qualities. Now I know that it protects against dark energy, and it feels that much more appropriate to be next to me while I sleep.

Top Crystals & Minerals for New Witches:

Below is a list of crystals or minerals with descriptions and magical properties. This list does not include all crystals and minerals, nor are they all required for magical rituals. It should be noted that different practitioners may have different perspectives on the magical properties—and that is okay. Focus more on your intention for the crystal and consider the magical properties as only a suggestion or starting point.

Red Jasper

Category: Crystal

Description: Red Jasper is a microcrystalline variety of quartz known for its deep red colour, often with streaks or patterns.

Magical Properties: It is grounding, stable, and strong. It is used to promote endurance and can be a great aid in balancing emotional energies.

Smoky Quartz

Category: Crystal

Description: Smoky Quartz is a translucent brown or grey variety of quartz. The colour ranges from light grey to deep black.

Magical Properties: Grounding, protection, and detoxification. It is believed to help dispel negative energies and aid in emotional healing.

Carnelian

Category: Crystal

Description: Carnelian is a variety of chalcedony that comes in colours ranging from pale orange to deep reddish-brown.

Magical Properties: Courage, vitality, and motivation. It is often used to boost confidence and stimulate creativity.

Orange Calcite

Category: Crystal

Description: Orange Calcite is a bright orange form of calcite, a common carbonate mineral.

Magical Properties: Creativity, energy, and emotional balance. It helps to cleanse the sacral chakra and remove stagnant energies.

Tiger's Eye

Category: Crystal

Description: Tiger's Eye is a metamorphic rock with a silky luster, typically golden to reddish-brown in colour.

Magical Properties: Protection, courage, and focus. It is known for its grounding energy and ability to provide mental clarity.

Citrine

Category: Crystal

Description: Citrine is a yellow variety of quartz, ranging from pale yellow to deep amber.

Magical Properties: Abundance, joy, and clarity. It is often called the "Merchant's Stone" for its believed ability to attract wealth and success.

Yellow Jasper

Category: Crystal

Description: Yellow Jasper is a variety of jasper characterized by its mustard yellow colour.

Magical Properties: Protection, clarity, and confidence. It helps to enhance mental focus and promote a positive outlook.

Rose Quartz

Category: Crystal

Description: Rose Quartz is a pink variety of quartz known for its soft, rosy hue.

Magical Properties: Love, compassion, and emotional healing. It is commonly used to promote self-love and harmonious relationships.

Green Aventurine

Category: Crystal

Description: Green Aventurine is a quartz variety containing mica or other minerals, giving it a shimmering quality.

Magical Properties: Luck, prosperity, and emotional calm. It is often associated with abundance and personal growth.

Rhodonite

Category: Crystal

Description: Rhodonite is a pink to red crystal, often with black manganese oxide veins.

Magical Properties: Emotional healing, forgiveness, and compassion. It is believed to help heal emotional wounds and promote love.

Blue Lace Agate

Category: Crystal

Description: Blue Lace Agate is a pale blue crystal with delicate, lace-like banding.

Magical Properties: Communication, calmness, and peace. It helps to soothe emotions and encourages clear, gentle communication.

Lapis Lazuli

Category: Crystal

Description: Lapis Lazuli is a deep blue metamorphic rock containing lazurite, often with pyrite inclusions.

Magical Properties: Wisdom, truth, and intuition. It is used to enhance intellectual abilities and stimulate spiritual insight.

Aquamarine

Category: Crystal

Description: Aquamarine is a blue or turquoise variety of beryl, often transparent and clear.

Magical Properties: Clarity, courage, and communication. It is associated with calming energies and enhancing verbal expression.

Amethyst

Category: Crystal

Description: Amethyst is a purple variety of quartz ranging from light lavender to deep violet.

Magical Properties: Protection, intuition, and spiritual growth. It is known for its calming and protective qualities.

Clear Quartz

Category: Crystal

Description: Clear Quartz is a transparent or translucent quartz crystal.

Magical Properties: Amplification, clarity, and energy. It is considered a master healer and can amplify the energies of other crystals.

Selenite

Category: Crystal

Description: Selenite is a transparent or translucent form of gypsum with a pearly luster.

Magical Properties: Clarity, purification, and spiritual connection. It is often used to cleanse other crystals and clear negative energies.

Sodalite

Category: Crystal

Description: Sodalite is a deep blue crystal with white veining.

Magical Properties: Logic, truth, and intuition. It helps to enhance mental clarity and deepen intuitive abilities.

Fluorite

Category: Crystal

Description: Fluorite comes in a variety of colours, often displaying multi-coloured patterns.

Magical Properties: Focus, protection, and clarity. It is known for its ability to clear mental fog and provide structure to thoughts.

Moonstone

Category: Crystal

Description: Moonstone is a feldspar mineral with a pearly and opalescent sheen, often white, peach, or blue.

Magical Properties: Intuition, emotional balance, and new beginnings. It is linked to the divine feminine and cycles of the moon.

Serpentine

Category: Crystal

Description: Serpentine is a green, patterned stone often mistaken for jade.

Magical Properties: Transformation, healing, and protection. It is believed to help release fear and assist in spiritual exploration and protection from dark energies.

Hematite

Category: Mineral

Description: Hematite is an iron oxide mineral known for its metallic luster and silver-gray to black colour.

Magical Properties: It is grounding, protective, and strong. It anchors energies and protects against negativity.

Pyrite

Category: Mineral

Description: Pyrite, also known as "Fool's Gold," is an iron sulfide mineral with a shiny, brass-yellow colour.

Magical Properties: abundance, protection, and confidence. It is believed to attract abundance and protect against negative energy.

These crystals and minerals have unique properties and energies that can enhance various aspects of magical practices and personal growth. They can be used in spellwork, meditation, or as talismans to support different intentions and energies.

Salt in Spellcrafting the Ultimate Mineral

Salt is a naturally occurring mineral composed primarily of sodium chloride. It can be found in various forms, including rock salt, sea salt, and table salt. Each type has unique characteristics and energy properties.

Magical Properties

Salt is renowned in magical practices for its ability to cleanse, purify, and protect. It is often used to create a barrier against negative energies and to purify spaces, objects, or people. Additionally, salt can be used in rituals for grounding and enhancing the clarity of one's intentions. Its purifying qualities make it a staple in many rituals, especially those involving protection, banishing, and consecration.

Uses in Spellcrafting

Purification: Sprinkle salt around a space or mix it with water for a cleansing wash to remove negative energies.

Protection: Salt can be used to create protective circles or barriers. For example, a ring of salt around a ritual space can prevent unwanted energies from entering.

Banishing: Salt is commonly used in spells to banish negative influences or spirits. It can be scattered across thresholds or mixed with herbs for a more potent banishing blend.

Grounding: Adding salt to a ritual bath or placing a small dish of salt in a room can help ground and stabilize energies.

Types of Salt

Sea Salt

Description: Harvested from evaporated seawater, sea salt retains trace minerals, which can enhance its energetic properties.

Magical Uses: Sea salt is often preferred for its natural and holistic qualities. It is commonly used in purification baths, rituals, and for cleansing crystals.

Preference: Many practitioners prefer sea salt for its natural origin and additional mineral content, which can add to its energetic potency.

Table Salt (Sodium Chloride)

Description: Table salt is refined and often contains anti-caking agents. It may also be iodized.

Magical Uses: While table salt is more processed, it is still effective for protective and purifying rituals. It is convenient for everyday use, such as sprinkling around a space for protection.

Preference: Table salt is more readily available and inexpensive, making it accessible quickly and practically. However, some practitioners prefer less processed options like sea salt for spiritual work.

Himalayan Pink Salt

Description: Mined from ancient seabeds in the Himalayas, this salt is known for its pink hue, which comes from trace minerals.

Magical Uses: It is often used for purification, grounding, and enhancing positive energy. It is also believed to help balance the chakras and clear negative energy from a space.

Epsom Salt (Magnesium Sulphate)

Description: A mineral compound made up of magnesium, sulphur, and oxygen. It is often used in bath soaks.

Magical Uses: Used for relaxation, stress relief, and enhancing mental clarity. It's also believed to help with physical and emotional healing.

Black Salt

Description: A type of salt that is either naturally occurring or made by combining sea salt with activated charcoal or other dark ingredients.

Magical Uses: It is commonly used in protection spells, banishing, and reversing negative energy. It is thought to absorb and neutralize harmful energies.

Hawaiian Red Alaea Salt

Description: A traditional Hawaiian salt infused with red clay, giving it a distinctive reddish-brown colour.

Magical Uses: Used for purification, grounding, and enhancing protection. Rituals also use it to honour the Earth and connect with ancestral energies.

Kosher Salt

Description: Coarse-grained salt commonly used in koshering meats due to its ability to draw out blood.

Magical Uses: It is used in purification and protection spells. Its coarse grains make it effective in creating salt circles and barriers.

Fleur de Sel

Description: A type of sea salt that forms as a thin crust on the surface of salt ponds, known for its delicate, flaky texture.

Magical Uses: It is often used in rituals for abundance, luxury, and spiritual elevation. Its delicate nature is thought to enhance the quality of magical workings.

Himalayan Black Salt (Kala Namak)

Description: A type of volcanic rock salt with a dark colour and unique flavour, commonly used in South Asian cuisine.

Magical Uses: It is used for protection and grounding. Its complex flavour and colour make it suitable for deepening spells related to transformation and personal growth.

Sole (Salt Sole)

Description: A saturated solution of salt and water, often made with Himalayan pink salt.

Magical Uses: It cleanses spaces and objects, enhances energy, and balances chakras. It is also used to charge crystals and other magical tools.

Dead Sea Salt

Description: It is harvested from the Dead Sea, which is known for its high mineral content, including magnesium, potassium, and calcium.

Magical Uses: It is used for deep cleansing, healing, and rejuvenation. Its mineral-rich composition makes it ideal for rituals focused on health and wellness.

Rock Salt

Description: Mined from underground deposits, often in large, crystalline chunks.

Magical Uses: It is used for protection, grounding, and creating protective barriers. Its raw, natural form makes it suitable for earth-based rituals and spellcrafting.

Each type of salt has unique properties and energies, and selecting the right one for your spellcrafting can enhance the effectiveness of your magical work.

Choosing Between Sea Salt and Table Salt

The choice between sea salt and table salt often comes down to preference and intention. Sea salt is favoured for its natural composition and holistic qualities, making it a popular choice for more refined spiritual practices. However, table salt is perfectly suitable for most magical purposes, especially when sea salt is not readily available. The intention behind the use of salt is more important than the type, and both can be powerful tools in a witch's practice.

The Shapes and Cuts of Crystals and Minerals in Spellcrafting

Crystals and minerals come in a variety of shapes and cuts, each carrying unique energies and purposes in spellcrafting. A crystal's shape can amplify, direct, or focus its inherent properties, making it a valuable tool for practitioners. Here, we'll explore some of the most common shapes and how they can be used in magical practices.

Raw/Natural

Raw crystals are uncut and unpolished, maintaining their natural form. These stones are powerful because they keep their full, untapped potential, directly connecting to the earth's energies. Raw crystals are often used for grounding, purification, and natural energy work. Their untamed nature makes them ideal for rituals that involve channeling earth energies or manifesting raw, primal forces.

Tumbled Stones

Tumbled stones are smooth, polished stones that are easy to carry and work with. Their polished surfaces make them comfortable to hold during meditation or to carry as a talisman. Tumbled stones are excellent for personal use, such as carrying in a pocket or placing in a sacred space to bring gentle, balanced energy. They are also commonly used in grid work, where their uniform shape and smooth edges allow for easy placement.

Points

Points have a naturally or artificially shaped end that comes to a point, directing energy outward or inward, depending on how they are oriented. Single-terminated points have one pointed end and are used to direct energy flow, either releasing negative energy or focusing positive energy into a specific area. Double-terminated points have two pointed ends, making them excellent for energy transmission and communication, as they can channel energy in two directions simultaneously.

Clusters

Clusters comprise multiple crystal points growing together from a common base. They radiate energy outward in all directions, making them powerful for cleansing and charging a space. Clusters can amplify the energy of a room or altar, clear negative energies, and support group rituals. Their collective energy makes them ideal for promoting harmony and cooperation.

Spheres

Spheres are polished, round crystals that emit energy equally in all directions. They are symbolic of completeness, unity, and infinity. Spheres are often used in meditation to promote balance and harmony, as their shape encourages the flow of energy in all directions. They can also be placed on altars or in a living space to promote a calm and peaceful environment.

Pyramids

Pyramids are crystals shaped into a pyramid form, which is believed to amplify and focus energies through the apex. This shape is useful for manifestation work, as it channels energy upwards to connect with higher realms. Pyramids can also enhance the power of other stones, charge objects, or protect a space by placing them at the center of a crystal grid.

Obelisks and Towers

Obelisks and towers are elongated stones with a pointed tip. They focus and amplify energy, directing it upward. These shapes are excellent for raising a space's vibration or grounding during meditation. They can also be placed in the center of a room to draw in and distribute energy or at the corners of a room to create an energetic boundary.

Hearts

Heart-shaped crystals are commonly used for emotional healing and love spells. The heart shape amplifies the crystal's energy towards love, compassion, and emotional well-being. These stones are often carried close to the heart, placed on an altar, or used in rituals to attract or heal love.

Cubes

Cubes are associated with stability, grounding, and protection. They represent the four elements and the four directions, making them powerful for grounding rituals and protection grids. Cubes can be placed in each corner of a room to create a stable, protective environment or carried for personal grounding and security.

Eggs

Egg-shaped crystals symbolize new beginnings, fertility, and potential. They are used in spells and rituals focused on growth, transformation, and creativity. The egg shape promotes a gentle flow of energy and can be used in meditations to connect with the energy of new life or to nurture a new project or idea.

Wands

Crystal wands are elongated and often tapered at one or both ends. They are powerful tools for directing energy, healing, and intention setting. Wands can cleanse the aura, direct energy during a ritual, or focus healing energy on a specific area. The shape of a wand allows the practitioner to channel and direct the crystal's energy with precision.

By understanding the unique properties of these different shapes and cuts, teen witches can select the most appropriate form of crystal for their magical needs. Whether it's for meditation, protection, healing, or manifestation, each shape offers a distinct way to work with the energies of the earth, enhancing both the effectiveness and intentionality of their spellcrafting.

Crystal Grid Layout: Sacred Geometry

Crystal grid layouts are versatile and powerful tools in crystal magic. They offer a structured yet flexible way to work with crystal energies. Whether for healing, manifestation, or spiritual growth, these grids can be a beautiful and meaningful addition to your practice.

Sacred geometry patterns are often used in crystal grids to amplify and direct the energy of the crystals. These patterns, each with unique properties and symbolism, can enhance the intentions and outcomes of crystal work.

Common Sacred Geometry Grids:

Vesica Piscis

Description: The Vesica Piscis comprises two overlapping circles, with the intersection representing a portal or a place of creation. This shape is often associated with balance, unity, and the intersection of the spiritual and physical worlds.

Number of Crystals: One central crystal, additional placement if required by the spellcaster.

Uses: Practitioners use the Vesica Piscis for intention setting, spells requiring balanced energy, or healing work.

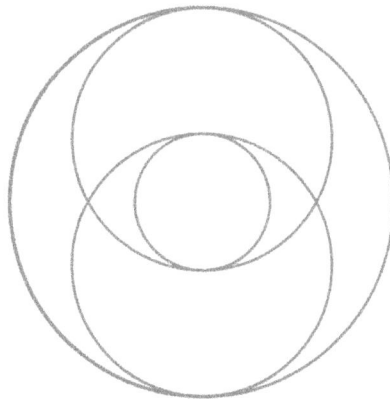

Hexagram (Star of David)

Description: A six-pointed star formed by two overlapping triangles. It symbolizes balance, harmony, and the integration of opposites.

Number of Crystals: Generally uses one central crystal, with crystals placed at each of the six points.

Uses: Ideal for balancing energies, protection, and spiritual connection. It's often used to align body, mind, and spirit or to harmonize relationships.

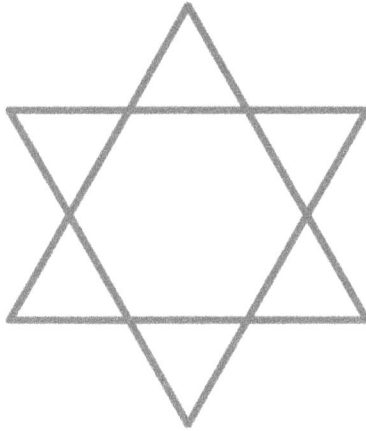

Metatron's Cube

Description: A complex figure consisting of 13 circles connected by lines. It contains every shape in the universe, making it a symbol of the creation and flow of energy.

Number of Crystals: Typically requires one central crystal, with additional crystals at the points and intersections of the 13 circles.

Uses: Powerful for healing, transformation, and connecting with higher realms. It can also be used for manifesting complex intentions or multidimensional healing.

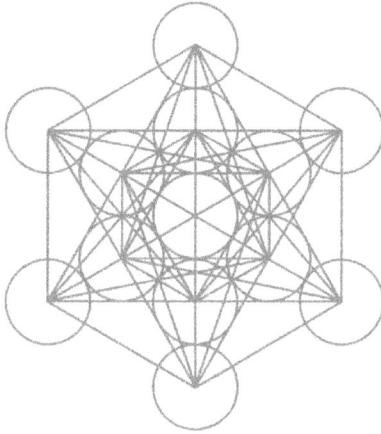

Sri Yantra

Description: A geometrical pattern composed of nine interlocking triangles, radiating from a central point, enclosed within two circles and a square. It represents the cosmos and the body.

Number of Crystals: Usually involves one central crystal, with additional crystals placed at key intersections or points within the pattern.

Uses: It is often used for meditation, spiritual enlightenment, and balancing masculine and feminine energies. It can help manifest desires and align with cosmic energies.

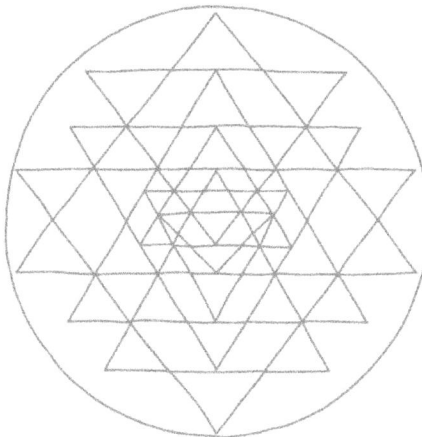

Pentagram

Description: A five-pointed star, often within a circle. It symbolizes the elements (earth, air, fire, water, and spirit) and protection.

Number of Crystals: Typically requires one central crystal, with crystals at each of the five points.

Uses: It is commonly used for protection, invoking elemental energies, and grounding. It's also associated with personal power and spiritual balance.

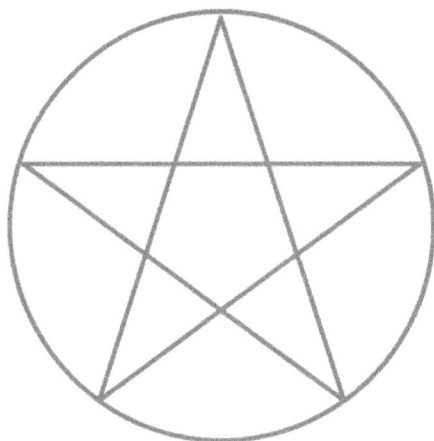

Spiral

Description: A continuous curve that radiates out from a central point, symbolizing growth, evolution, and the cycle of life.

Number of Crystals: This can vary, but typically starts with a central crystal and spirals outward, with crystals placed along the spiral path.

Uses: It is great for healing, personal growth, and transformation. It can also be used to align with the natural flow of life and cosmic cycles.

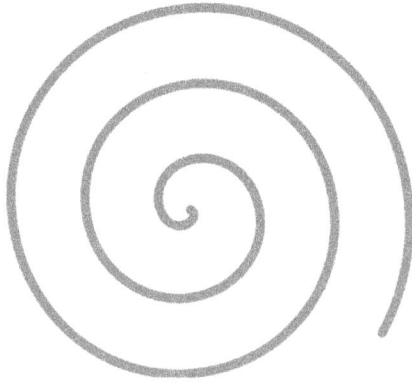

Double Spiral (Infinity)

Description: Two intertwined spirals symbolize eternity and the universe's infinite nature.

Number of Crystals: Often uses one central crystal, with crystals placed along the spirals. The number can vary based on the design's complexity.

Uses: Ideal for working with infinite possibilities, continuity, and deep spiritual connections. It can help with breaking old patterns and embracing new cycles.

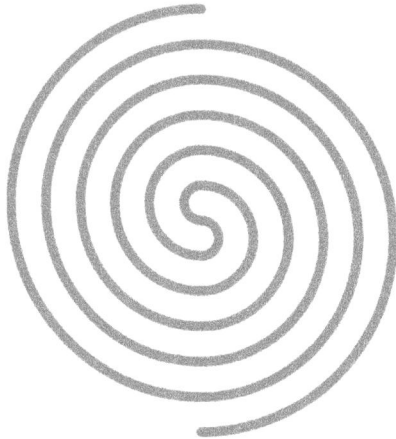

Flower of Life

Description: The Flower of Life is a complex geometric pattern composed of multiple overlapping circles, forming a flower-like design. It symbolizes creation, the interconnectedness of life, and the universe's blueprint.

Number of Crystals: One central crystal, potentially six or more additional crystals at the outer or inner intersections.

Uses: Practitioners can use the Flower of Life layout for manifesting goals, as it represents the infinite potential and interconnectedness of all things. It is also leveraged when trying to amplify intentions and spiritual growth.

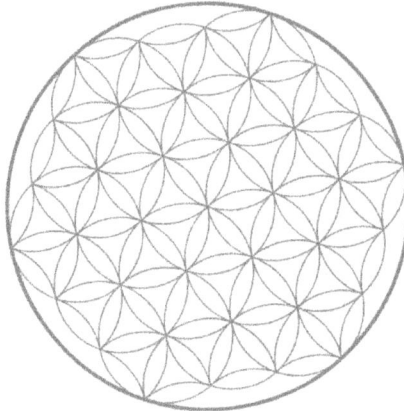

Seed of Life

Description: The Seed of Life is made up of seven overlapping circles, forming a flower-like pattern. It is a subset of the Flower of Life and represents creation, fertility, and the interconnectedness of life.

Number of Crystals: Typically requires one central crystal and six surrounding crystals.

Uses: This pattern is often used for new beginnings, growth, and setting intentions. It's an excellent way to plant the "seeds" of new projects or goals.

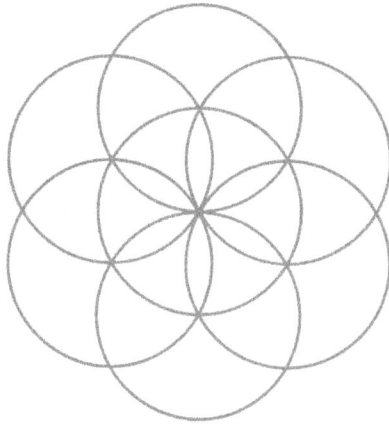

How to Use Crystal Grid Layouts:

Select Crystals: Choose crystals that align with your intention. For example, rose quartz is for love, citrine is for abundance, and amethyst is for spiritual growth.

Cleanse Crystals: Before placing them on the grid, cleanse the crystals to remove any negative energies. This can be done with moonlight, sunlight, or a cleansing ritual.

Set Up the Grid: Lay out the chosen pattern on a flat surface. You can use a printed grid, a drawn pattern, or even a cloth with the design. The layout serves as a guide for placing the crystals.

Place Crystals: Start by placing a central stone, often called the "master crystal," which anchors the grid's energy. Then, place additional crystals around the master crystal according to the chosen layout. Each crystal's placement should be intentional, based on its properties and the desired outcome.

Activate the Grid: Once the crystals are placed, activate the grid by connecting the crystals energetically. This can be done by using a wand, finger, or another crystal to trace lines between the stones, visualizing the energy flowing between them. Focus on your intention during this process.

Set an Intention: Clearly state or write your intention, infusing the grid with purpose. This can be a silent or spoken affirmation, or a written note placed beneath the central stone.

Meditate or Focus: Spend time in meditation or contemplation with the grid, connecting with the energies of the crystals and the layout. Visualize your intention manifesting and feel the energy of the grid supporting your goal.

Maintain the Grid: Leave the grid in place for as long as necessary, checking in periodically to refresh the energy or adjust the crystals as needed. Some practitioners like to cleanse and reactivate their grids regularly.

Deactivating the Grid: When the grid has served its purpose, deactivate it by thanking the crystals and removing them from the layout. Cleanse the crystals before storing them.

General Guidelines for Using Crystal Grids with Sacred Geometry

Choose the Right Pattern: Select a pattern that aligns with your intention. Each shape has its unique energy, so choose one that resonates with your goal, whether it's healing, protection, manifestation, or spiritual growth.

Number of Crystals: While some patterns suggest specific numbers of crystals, you can adapt based on your needs. The key is to place crystals at significant points within the pattern to create a flow of energy.

Central Crystal: Most grids use a central crystal, often called the "master crystal," which anchors the grid's energy. This crystal is usually larger or more significant than the others and is chosen based on the primary intention.

Activation: After setting up your grid, activate it by connecting the crystals energetically. This can be done with a wand, another crystal, or simply by visualizing the energy flowing between them.

Focus and Meditation: Focus on your grid, meditating, and visualizing your intention. The geometric pattern and crystals work together to amplify and direct the energy towards your goal.

Maintenance: Keep the grid in place as long as needed, and regularly check in to refresh the energy or make adjustments. Cleanse the crystals periodically to maintain their energetic purity.

Ethical Considerations: Always consider the ethical sourcing of your crystals and respect the cultural origins of the sacred geometry you are using.

By carefully selecting and arranging crystals in these sacred geometric patterns, practitioners can create powerful tools for transformation, healing, and spiritual growth.

Incorporating Crystals into Rituals:

The wonderful thing about working with crystals is that you don't have to "do" anything—simply keeping them close by allows their healing energies to influence your energy field. Try placing a crystal in the areas of your home where you spend the most time. You can also hold a crystal during meditation or breathwork exercises to infuse your practice with an extra dose of magic.

Alternatives to Crystals and Minerals

Like the prior chapter on herbs and flowers, you can represent your crystal or mineral using an alternative or proxy. The written name of the crystal or mineral can be leveraged, as can a painting or drawing.

Practitioners should avoid plastic or artificial crystals and minerals. Practitioners should also know some stores will try to sell plastic as a genuine item. Like herbs and flowers, plastic is not a renewable or environmentally friendly resource and is counterproductive to your witch magic.

Sea Glass and River Stone as Creative Alternatives

Sea glass and river stones can be incorporated into magical practices as alternatives to crystals and minerals. While they might not have the same traditional associations as specific crystals, they offer unique qualities and symbolism that can be valuable in spellcrafting and ritual work.

Sea Glass

Description: Sea glass is smooth, frosted glass tumbled by the ocean. It often comes in various colours and is found along beaches.
   Magical Uses:
   Healing and Transformation: The process of sea glass being smoothed by the sea can symbolize healing, personal transformation, and the smoothing of rough edges in one's life.
   Emotional Release: The ocean's power to cleanse and transform glass can be seen as a metaphor for releasing emotional burdens and rejuvenating the spirit.

Connection to the Ocean: Sea glass can be used in spells or rituals that aim to connect with the energies of the ocean, such as for relaxation, cleansing, or enhancing intuition. It can represent a water element.

River Stones

Description: River stones are smooth, rounded stones worn down by rivers' flowing water. They come in various sizes and colours.

Magical Uses:

Grounding and Stability: River stones are often used for grounding, as their smoothness and connection to the Earth can help bring balance and stability.

Flow and Adaptability: The stones' smooth, worn appearance symbolizes adaptability and the ability to go with the flow, making them useful for spells related to change and flexibility.

Connection to Nature: River stones represent both earth and water elements, and they can enhance one's connection to natural energies, support physical health, or promote a sense of peace and calm.

Incorporating Sea Glass and River Stones into Magic

Personal Touch: Sea glass and river stones can be chosen for their personal significance or aesthetic qualities, adding a unique and meaningful element to spell work.

Altar Decorations: They can enhance water, nature, and transformation energies by being used as altar decorations or in ritual spaces.

Meditation Tools: Both can be used as focal points during meditation to connect with their elemental energies and symbolic meanings.

Using sea glass and river stones offers a way to work with natural materials shaped by nature's forces, making them powerful tools for connecting with Earth's energies and personal growth.

Chapter 8

CRYSTALS AND CHAKRAS

Welcome to the fascinating world of chakras and crystals! Chakras are energy centres in the body, each associated with different physical, emotional, and spiritual aspects of our lives. When these chakras are balanced, we feel more harmonious and at peace. Crystals, with their unique vibrations, can help align and balance these chakras, enhancing our overall well-being. In this chapter, we'll explore the seven main chakras, their locations, symbols, associated crystals, and the purpose of each chakra.

Root Chakra (Muladhara)

Location: Base of the spine
  Symbol: Four-petaled lotus
  Colour: Red
  Associated Crystals: Red Jasper, Hematite, Smoky Quartz
  Purpose: The Root Chakra is all about stability, security, and our basic needs. It's the foundation of our physical and emotional existence, grounding us in reality. When balanced, we feel safe, secure, and confident. Teens may focus on this chakra to feel more secure in their environment, especially during times of change or uncertainty.

Sacral Chakra (Svadhisthana)

Location: Lower abdomen, about two inches below the navel
    Symbol: Six-petaled lotus
    Colour: Orange
    Associated Crystals: Carnelian, Orange Calcite, Tiger's Eye
    Purpose: The Sacral Chakra is the center of creativity, pleasure, and emotions. It governs our relationships with others and our ability to experience joy. Balancing this chakra helps with self-expression and emotional well-being. Teens may work with this chakra to explore their creativity and form healthy emotional connections.

Solar Plexus Chakra (Manipura)

Location: Upper abdomen, around the stomach area
    Symbol: Ten-petaled lotus
    Colour: Yellow
    Associated Crystals: Citrine, Yellow Jasper, Pyrite
    Purpose: The Solar Plexus Chakra is the seat of personal power, confidence, and self-esteem. It's all about asserting yourself and taking control of your life. When balanced, you feel motivated and capable of achieving your goals. Teens

may find this chakra helpful for building self-confidence and setting personal boundaries.

Heart Chakra (Anahata)

Location: Centre of the chest
  Symbol: Twelve-petaled lotus
  Colour: Green or Pink
  Associated Crystals: Rose Quartz, Green Aventurine, Rhodonite
Purpose: The Heart Chakra is the center of love, compassion, and kindness. It governs our ability to love ourselves and others. A balanced Heart Chakra fosters forgiveness, empathy, and deep connections. Teens can focus on this chakra to cultivate self-love and improve relationships with friends and family.

Throat Chakra (Vishuddha)

Location: Throat area
  Symbol: Sixteen-petaled lotus
  Colour: Blue
  Associated Crystals: Blue Lace Agate, Lapis Lazuli, Aquamarine
Purpose: The Throat Chakra is associated with communication, expression, and truth. It enables us to speak our truth and express our thoughts and feelings clearly. Balancing this chakra helps with effective communication and listening.

Teens may work on this chakra to improve their ability to express themselves and communicate openly.

Third Eye Chakra (Ajna)

Location: Forehead, between the eyebrows
  Symbol: Two-petaled lotus
  Colour: Indigo
  Associated Crystals: Amethyst, Sodalite, Fluorite
  Purpose: The Third Eye Chakra is the center of intuition, insight, and wisdom. It helps us see beyond the physical and understand deeper truths. When balanced, this chakra enhances intuition and inner guidance. Teens may focus on this chakra to develop their intuition and gain clarity in decision-making.

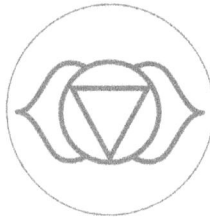

Crown Chakra (Sahasrara)

Location: Top of the head
  Symbol: Thousand-petaled lotus
  Colour: Violet or White
  Associated Crystals: Clear Quartz, Selenite, Amethyst
  Purpose: The Crown Chakra represents our connection to the divine and the universe. It is the source of spiritual awareness and enlightenment. A balanced Crown Chakra helps us feel connected to a higher purpose and the greater good.

Teens may focus on this chakra to explore spirituality and find a sense of meaning in life.

Using Crystals to Balance Chakras

You can meditate with the crystal, wear it as jewellery, or place it on the corresponding chakra location during relaxation to work with crystals and chakras. For example, to balance your Heart Chakra, you might hold a piece of Rose Quartz over your heart or wear it as a necklace. Visualize the colour of the chakra filling your body and imagine the crystal's energy harmonizing the chakra.

Creating a Chakra Crystal Set

Creating a chakra crystal set is a fun way to start working with these energies. You can collect a crystal for each chakra, such as:

1. Root Chakra: Red Jasper
2. Sacral Chakra: Tiger's Eye
3. Solar Plexus Chakra: Citrine
4. Heart Chakra: Rose Quartz
5. Throat Chakra: Blue Lace Agate
6. Third Eye Chakra: Amethyst
7. Crown Chakra: Clear Quartz

Keep these crystals in a special box or pouch and use them to balance your energy.

Key Takeaway

Chakras and crystals offer a beautiful way to explore your inner world and enhance your well-being. As a teenager, you're navigating many changes and challenges, and understanding these energy centres can help you find balance and peace. Remember, the journey of working with chakras and crystals is personal and unique to everyone. Take your time, explore different practices, and trust your intuition. Whether you're seeking to boost your confidence, enhance creativity, or find inner calm, the world of chakras and crystals is a magical realm to discover.

Chapter 9

THE MAGIC OF COLOURS IN SPELLCRAFTING

C olour is a powerful tool in magic and spellcrafting, offering a visual and symbolic way to enhance intentions and connect with specific energies. In many magical traditions, colours are believed to carry distinct vibrations that align with particular purposes. For teenagers exploring magic, understanding the meanings and uses of different colours can add a vibrant dimension to their practice. This chapter will guide you through the symbolic meanings of colours and how to incorporate them into your spells and rituals.

Red: Energy, Passion, and Courage

Representation: Red is a dynamic colour representing energy, passion, courage, and strength. It is associated with fire and the element of Mars.

Uses in Spell Craft: Use red in spells to boost confidence, attract love, or increase physical vitality. Red can also be used for protection spells and to ignite motivation.

Items: Red ribbon, red flowers, red crystals (such as garnet or ruby), red clothing.

Orange: Creativity, Joy, and Success

Representation: Orange combines the energy of red with the cheerfulness of yellow. It symbolizes creativity, joy, enthusiasm, and success.

Uses in Spellcraft: Incorporate orange in spells to enhance creativity, bring joy, or attract success in endeavours. It's also useful for spells related to ambition and career growth.

Items: Orange candles (battery-operated for safety), orange flowers (such as marigolds), orange crystals (like carnelian), and orange paper.

Yellow: Clarity, Communication, and Intellect

Representation: Yellow is associated with the sun, representing clarity, communication, intellect, and happiness. It resonates with the element of air.

Uses in Spellcraft: Use yellow in spells to improve mental clarity, enhance communication, boost memory, and bring joy. It's also helpful for spells involving study and learning.

Items: Yellow fabrics, yellow flowers (like sunflowers), yellow crystals (such as citrine), yellow journals for writing, yellow tea cup.

Green: Growth, Healing, and Abundance

Representation: Green symbolizes nature, growth, healing, and abundance. It is linked to the heart chakra and the element of earth.

Uses in Spellcraft: Green is ideal for spells related to healing, personal growth, prosperity, and fertility. It can also ground and balance energy.

Items: Green plants, green crystals (like aventurine or jade), green cloth, green pen for writing intentions.

Blue: Calm, Protection, and Spirituality

Representation: Blue represents calm, protection, and spirituality. It is connected to water and the throat chakra and is often associated with tranquillity and peace.

Uses in Spellcraft: Use blue in spells for emotional healing, enhancing intuition, promoting calm, and spiritual growth. It's also effective in protective spells and for clear communication.

Items: Blue stones (such as lapis lazuli or turquoise), blue water (coloured with safe food dye), blue clothing, and blue fabric for altar clothes, blue ribbon.

Purple: Wisdom, Psychic Ability, and Spiritual Power

Representation: Purple symbolizes wisdom, psychic ability, and spiritual power. It is often linked to the crown chakra and the element of spirit.

Uses in Spellcraft: Incorporate purple into spells to enhance psychic abilities, connect with spiritual guides, and seek wisdom. It's also used for meditation and spiritual protection.

Items: Purple crystals (like amethyst), purple fabric, purple ink, lavender flowers.

Pink: Love, Compassion, and Friendship

Representation: Pink is the colour of love, compassion, and friendship. It carries the gentle and nurturing aspects of red.

Uses in Spellcraft: Use pink in spells to attract love, strengthen friendships, promote self-love, and encourage compassion. It's also beneficial for healing emotional wounds.

Items: Pink roses, pink quartz, pink fabric, pink paint for art-based spells.

White: Purity, Protection, and Clarity

Representation: White represents purity, protection, and clarity. It is considered the colour of the divine and is linked to all elements.

Uses in Spellcraft: White can be used in any spell as it is a universal colour that can substitute for any other. It is good for purification, protection, and clarity. It is also used in rituals for new beginnings.

Items: White flowers (such as lilies), crystals (like clear quartz), fabric, and feathers.

Black: Protection, Banishing, and Transformation

Representation: Black symbolizes protection, banishing, and transformation. It is often associated with mystery, the night, and the unknown.

Uses in Spellcraft: Use black in spells to protect against negative energy, banish unwanted influences, or during times of transformation. It's also effective in grounding and shadow work.

Items: Black stones (such as obsidian or onyx), black fabric, and black ink for writing banishing spells.

Brown: Stability, Home, and Animal Magic

Representation: Brown represents stability, home, and the natural world. It is connected to the earth and is often used in animal and nature spells.

Uses in Spellcraft: Brown is used in spells to ground, enhance stability, and strengthen connections to home and family. It's also used in animal magic and to connect with nature spirits.

Items: Brownstones (like tiger's eye), earth or soil, brown fabric, animal totems, or figurines.

Incorporating Colours into Spellcraft

To integrate colours into your spell craft, consider the following methods:

Clothing and Accessories: Wear clothing or accessories in the colour corresponding to your intention to carry that energy with you throughout the day.

Altar Decorations: Decorate your altar with items of colour that match your spell's intention. This can include clothes, stones, flowers, and other symbolic objects.

Coloured Paper and Ink: Write your spells, affirmations, or intentions on coloured paper with matching ink. The colour will amplify the energy of your words.

Visualizations: During meditations or spells, visualize the colour associated with your intention surrounding you, filling you with the desired energy.

Art and Crafts: Create art or crafts in the colours that represent your spell's purpose. This can be a fun and creative way to channel your intentions.

Remember, the key to successful spell crafting is your intention and focus. While colours can enhance and amplify your spells, the most important component is your belief and energy. Experiment with different colours and see how they affect your magic and personal energy. As you grow in your practice, you may find that certain colours resonate more with you than others, guiding you on your unique magical journey.

Chapter 10

THE MAGIC OF SELF-EXPRESSION

I magine having a secret language, one that only you can understand. A way to express your deepest feelings, wildest dreams, and most powerful desires. That's the magic of self-expression, and it's a spell you can cast anytime, anywhere and in numerous formats.

When you let your creativity flow—through art, writing, or any other outlet—you tap into a part of yourself that's pure and authentic. It's like opening a portal to your inner world, where anything is possible. The best part? There are no rules, no limits, and no one to judge you.

Think of self-expression as your personal superpower. When you create something from your heart, you infuse it with your energy and intentions. It becomes a symbol of who you are and what you stand for. And just like a magic wand, it has the power to transform your life and the world around you.

Personal Sigils and Symbols: Crafting Your Unique Magic

One way to harness the power of self-expression is by creating your own personal symbols and sigils. A sigil is a visual representation of your desires and goals, crafted from a unique combination of letters or symbols with special meaning. When you create a sigil, you're planting a seed of intention that can grow and manifest in your life.

How to Create a Sigil-General Overview

In the next chapter, we will go into more depth on creating sigils, but the following is a general idea of the steps.

1. Define Your Intention: Start by clearly and concisely stating your desire or goal. This could be a single word or a phrase.

2. Simplify the Statement: Remove repeating letters to condense the statement into a unique set of characters.

3. Design Your Sigil: Arrange the remaining letters into a symbol that resonates with you. It can be abstract or stylized—what matters is that it feels right.

You can draw your sigil, paint it, or even stitch it onto clothing. Place it somewhere you'll see it often, like on your journal cover or as a wallpaper on your phone. This symbol constantly reminds you of your intention and helps you focus your energy on bringing it to fruition.

Storytelling and Personal Myth-Making

We all have stories within us waiting to be told. When you create your own myths and legends, you tap into the power of your imagination and shape your reality. Through storytelling, you can explore your experiences, dreams, and truths, giving them form and meaning.

You might write a short story, a poem, or even a song that reflects a significant moment in your life. These creative expressions can be powerful tools for self-discovery and healing. They allow you to process emotions, understand your journey, and connect with others who may share similar experiences.

The Therapeutic Power of Creative Expression

Evidence shows that engaging in creative activities can profoundly impact mental health and well-being. Art therapy, for example, can reduce symptoms of anxiety, depression, and stress while promoting self-awareness and emotional resilience. Writing has therapeutic benefits, helping people process experiences and find meaning in their lives.

Consider the different ways creativity and your personal expression can be incorporated into your witchcraft. It is easier to imagine incorporating drawing or painting, but there are other forms of self-expression. Consider writing a poem for use in a spell, vocal, or instrumental music. Gardening lends itself well to magic. But so does sculpture, mixed media, and even fashion. Your creative outlet can be part of your magical self-expression.

Inspirational Examples

Frida Kahlo: The renowned Mexican artist used her art to explore her identity and emotions despite facing numerous challenges, including chronic pain and disability. Her paintings, often depicting her experiences and struggles, became powerful symbols of resilience and self-acceptance. As Kahlo said, "I paint myself because I am so often alone and because I am the subject I know best."

Maya Angelou: The celebrated poet and civil rights activist used her writing to speak truth to power and give voice to marginalized communities' experiences. Her words, often drawing on her own life story, became a source of strength and inspiration for countless readers around the world.

How to Incorporate Self-Expression into Your Life

Daily Creative Practice: Set aside time each day for creative activities like drawing, writing, or making music. Even just 10-15 minutes can make a difference.

Journaling or Sketching: Keep a journal or sketchbook to freely express your thoughts and feelings without judgment.

Create a Sacred Space: Set up a personal altar or sacred space where you can display your sigils, symbols, and other meaningful objects.

Share Your Work: Share your creations with others through social media, local art shows, or with friends and family.

Learn New Skills: Seek opportunities to learn new creative skills, such as taking a pottery class or joining a writing group.

Remember, self-expression is not about perfection or pleasing others. It's about honoring your voice and vision. Let your inner light shine through, experiment without fear, and embrace the magic of your creativity.

What if you are just not that creative? That is okay. There is no rule that it has to be perfect, and sharing your work is just a suggestion. If you want to keep it personal that is okay. Be open to different forms of self-express and creativity and try new things.

Key Takeaways

Self-expression is a magical tool for personal growth and empowerment. By creating your own symbols, sigils, and stories, you tap into your inner wisdom and manifest your desires.

Engaging in creative activities can improve mental health, reduce stress, and promote emotional resilience.

Expressing yourself creatively helps you connect with your inner self and the world around you, leaving a lasting impact.

Chapter 11

THE ART OF SIGILS

The Power of a Name

As we learned in the previous chapter, a sigil is a design representing a word or phrase. What word is more powerful than your name? It doesn't have to be your assigned name; maybe it is an alternative that represents you.

Leveraging the same steps from the sigil instructions, a practitioner can create a sigil representing themselves. This can be added to spell pouches, the altar, or any other spellcasting steps.

Below are two examples. The first, we took the name SALLY and used an elaborate font. Instead of eliminating an L, we used both and layered them horizontally and one in reverse. This sigil not only represents our fictitious Sally, but the placement of the letters also emphasizes the word SAY. This could be meaningful if Sally wanted to work on empowering herself to speak up for herself or answer questions in class.

The second example is the name KIM. We reversed the K using a curved line, then a small horizontal line, the first part of the I. Then the M which is also created the straight line for the K. The sigil finishes with a small line for the second half of the I. It is not an elaborate sigil but could be done in one fluid motion.

Create a Sigil using a Wheel

A Sigil Wheel or Witches Wheel is a visual representation of the English alphabet arranged in three circles. A sigil is created by drawing a line or curve from one letter to the next. Like much of our magical practice, there is customization in the steps.

In the first example, we used the word LOVE. We started with the L, created a loop around the O and the V, and finished with a curved line down to the E. Because the O and the V are placed so close together, it forms a double loop.

In the second example, we took the unique letters in the word PROTEC-TION, P, R, O, T, E, C, I, N, and marked them on the wheel. We then used curved lines to connect them in order. You notice that moving from the C to the I required following the same path back from the E to the C, so we added a second smaller line to denote the movement.

The Witches Wheel works well for smaller words or phrases but can become messy if there are many unique letters.

Symbols in Sigil Creation

Another option for creating a sigil is to represent each letter by a symbol. Then, you can blend each symbol together to make a larger symbol. It is important to keep each letter symbol small and easy to work with and use a variety of shapes to provide plenty of options.

Define Your Intention: Start with a clear and specific intention. For our example, the intention is to become more confident in social situations.

Create a Statement: Write your intention in a present-tense, positive statement, "I am confident in social situations."

Remove Repeating Letters: Remove the repeating letters from the statement. We only need each letter once. For example, the statement above becomes: I, A, M, C, O, N, F, D, E, T, S, U

Create the Sigil: Using the unique letters, design an abstract symbol. There are no set rules for this part; the design should be personal and resonate with you. Alternatively, you could assign a symbol to each letter and then use the symbols in a design. For example, if 'I' is a dot, and 'A' is a half circle, you could add the dot inside the half circle.

Charge the Sigil: Once you've created your sigil, you need to charge it with your intention. This means focusing your energy and concentration on the sigil to infuse it with the desired outcome. Here's how you can do it:

Meditate: Find a quiet space and meditate while focusing on your sigil. Visualize yourself being confident in social situations. Imagine the feelings and experiences of this confidence.

Use Rituals: To enhance the charging process, you can incorporate rituals or symbols that resonate with you.

Energy Focus: Focus on the sigil and your intention, and allow yourself to be fully absorbed in the feeling of already achieving your goal.

Let Go: After charging your sigil, let go of the intention and avoid obsessing over it. Trust that the sigil will work on a subconscious level and help manifest your desire. The idea is to release your conscious focus on the intention and allow it to unfold naturally.

Integrate the Sigil: You can incorporate your sigil into your life in various ways:

Keep It Visible: Place the sigil somewhere you'll see it regularly, like in a journal or on a wall.

Artistic Items: Create jewelry or artwork featuring the sigil to keep its energy close.

Meditation: Use the sigil during meditation or when setting intentions.

By following these steps, you'll create a personal and powerful symbol that supports your goals and desires.

Chapter 12

LUNAR MAGIC

The moon has been a source of fascination and inspiration for centuries, especially in witchcraft. Its powerful influence on the tides and its consistent cycle make it a symbol of change, reflection, and renewal. For teenagers navigating the ups and downs of life, understanding and working with the phases of the moon can provide a unique way to manage emotions, set goals, and cultivate a positive outlook. Lunar magic isn't about controlling fate but about tuning into natural rhythms to enhance self-awareness and well-being.

The Eight Phases of the Moon

Understanding the phases of the moon and their symbolic meanings can help teens harness lunar energy for personal growth and mental health. Each phase offers a unique opportunity to engage in rituals or activities that align with the moon's energy.

New Moon: A Time for New Beginnings

- **Symbolism**: The new moon represents a fresh start, making it an ideal time for setting intentions and planting seeds for future growth.

- **Ritual/Activity: Intention-Setting Journal** – Write down your goals, dreams, or new habits you want to cultivate. Place these written intentions under a crystal or candle on your windowsill to absorb the moon's energy. You can also create a vision board with images and words that represent your goals.

Waxing Crescent: Building Energy and Momentum

- **Symbolism**: As the moon begins to grow, so does the energy around your intentions. This phase is about gathering momentum and putting plans into action.

- **Ritual/Activity**: **Crafting a Plan** – Create a step-by-step plan to achieve one of your goals. Break down your intention into actionable steps and set small, manageable tasks. You can also draw or doodle your progress to visualize your journey.

First Quarter: Taking Action

- **Symbolism**: The first quarter moon is a time of action and overcoming challenges. It's about making decisions and moving forward despite obstacles.

- **Ritual/Activity**: **Courage Charm** – Create a charm or talisman to remind you of your strength and resilience. This could be a bracelet, a small stone, or any object that holds personal significance. Hold the object in your hands, and as you focus on it, visualize yourself confidently facing challenges.

Waxing Gibbous: Refinement and Adjustment

- **Symbolism**: As the moon approaches fullness, this phase is about refining your plans and making necessary adjustments.

- **Ritual/Activity**: **Progress Check-In** – Reflect on your progress and make any needed changes. Write about what's working, what isn't, and how you can adjust your approach. Consider organizing your space or cleaning your room as a way to create a supportive environment for your goals.

Full Moon: Manifestation and Completion

- **Symbolism**: The full moon is a time of heightened energy, manifestation, and culmination of efforts.

- **Ritual/Activity: Full Moon Gratitude Ritual** – Gather outside or near a window with a good view of the moon. Write down things you are grateful for and any achievements you've made. Hold a small release ceremony by burning a piece of paper with anything negative you wish to let go of (safely and with adult supervision, if necessary). Celebrate with a small treat or fun activity to honor your hard work.

Waning Gibbous (Disseminating): Sharing and Gratitude

- **Symbolism**: After the full moon, this phase focuses on sharing knowledge, expressing gratitude, and giving back.

- **Ritual/Activity: Acts of Kindness** – Share your experiences or knowledge with others. This could be through a blog post, a social media update, or simply talking with friends. Practice acts of kindness, such as helping someone in need or volunteering your time. Reflect on what you've learned and express gratitude.

Last Quarter (Third Quarter): Release and Forgiveness

- **Symbolism**: This phase is about releasing what no longer serves you and practicing forgiveness.

- **Ritual/Activity: Forgiveness Meditation** – Find a quiet space and meditate on letting go of grudges or negative feelings. Visualize yourself releasing these emotions into the universe. You can also write a letter to yourself or someone else expressing forgiveness, then either keep it as a reminder or tear it up as a symbol of release.

Waning Crescent (Balsamic): Rest and Reflection

- **Symbolism**: The final phase of the lunar cycle is a time for rest, recuperation, and introspection.

- **Ritual/Activity**: **Self-Care Ritual** – Dedicate time to self-care activities such as taking a relaxing bath, practicing yoga, or journaling your thoughts and feelings. Reflect on the past lunar cycle, noting what you've learned and how you've grown. Plan some quiet time to recharge and prepare for the next new moon.

Unique Moons and Corresponding Rituals:

Blue Moon: Embracing Rare Opportunities

- **What It Is**: A blue moon occurs when there are two full moons in one calendar month. This rare event is often seen as a time of heightened energy and potential.

- **Ritual**: **Rare Opportunity Ritual** – Use the unique energy of the blue moon to focus on rare or special opportunities. Write down a unique goal or dream that feels challenging or unusual. Create a small altar with items that symbolize your aspirations (like crystals, meaningful objects, or symbols of your goal). Light a candle and spend time visualizing your unique goal coming to fruition, embracing the rare energy of the blue moon.

Black Moon: Deep Reflection and Shadow Work

- **What It Is**: A black moon is the second new moon in a single calendar month. It symbolizes a time for deep introspection and exploring the subconscious.

- **Ritual: Shadow Work Meditation** – Sit in a quiet, dimly lit space and meditate on aspects of yourself that you usually keep hidden. Reflect on any fears, insecurities, or unresolved emotions. Write down what you discover and consider ways to integrate these aspects into your life positively. You can also create a "shadow box" where you place symbols or items representing things you wish to acknowledge and transform.

Supermoon: Amplifying Intentions

- **What It Is**: A supermoon occurs when a full moon is closest to Earth, making it appear larger and brighter. It amplifies lunar energy.

- **Ritual: Amplification Ritual** – Use the powerful energy of a supermoon to amplify your intentions. On the night of the supermoon, create a crystal grid or a circle of candles. Place written intentions or affirmations in the center. Meditate on these intentions, visualizing them growing stronger and brighter, just like the supermoon. This is an ideal time to charge crystals or personal items with lunar energy.

Harvest Moon: Abundance and Gratitude

- **What It Is**: The full moon closest to the autumnal equinox, known as the Harvest Moon, is a time of abundance and reflection on the fruits of one's labor.

- **Ritual: Gratitude and Abundance Ritual** – Reflect on the abundance in your life and express gratitude. Create a gratitude journal entry or a list of things you are thankful for. If possible, gather natural items like leaves, acorns, or fruits to represent the harvest. Arrange these items on an altar or table as symbols of abundance. Light a candle and give thanks for all the blessings in your life, focusing on the positive aspects and what you've achieved.

Blood Moon: Transformation and Rebirth

- **What It Is**: A blood moon occurs during a total lunar eclipse when the moon takes on a reddish hue. It symbolizes transformation and rebirth.

- **Ritual: Transformation Ritual** – Embrace change and transformation. Write down old habits, beliefs, or aspects of your life that you wish to transform. During the eclipse, perform a symbolic act of transformation, such as burning the paper (safely) to signify letting go. As the eclipse ends, visualize yourself embracing new, positive changes. You can also create a piece of art that represents your transformation and rebirth.

Water Moon: Emotional Healing and Intuition

- **What It Is**: While not an official lunar phase, the concept of a "Water Moon" refers to the moon's influence on emotions and intuition, often associated with full moons in water signs (Cancer, Scorpio, Pisces).

- **Ritual: Emotional Healing Ritual** – Focus on emotional healing and nurturing your intuition. Set up a comfortable space with water elements, such as a bowl of water, seashells, or blue candles. Meditate or practice deep breathing while focusing on releasing emotional blockages. You can also write down any emotions you're struggling with and submerge the paper in water as a symbolic act of cleansing and letting go. Afterwards, spend time journaling or drawing to explore your intuitive insights.

By engaging with these unique moons and their corresponding rituals, teens can tap into powerful energies for personal growth, healing, and transformation. Each unique moon offers a chance to connect deeply with different aspects of life and the self, providing a rich tapestry of experiences to support mental and emotional well-being.

Chapter 13

RUNE MAGIC IN SPELLCRAFTING

R une magic is an ancient and powerful form of divination and spellcraft originating in Northern Europe. The runic alphabet, also known as the Elder Futhark, comprises symbols, each with its own meaning and magical properties. Runes offers new witches a versatile and creative way to enhance spellcasting and connect with ancient traditions. This chapter will introduce the basics of rune magic, how to use runes in spells, and a summary of different runes and their meanings.

Runes can be used in various ways within spellcraft:

Divination: Like tarot cards, runes can be cast or drawn to gain insight into a question or situation.

Amulets and Talismans: Carve or draw runes onto objects like stones, wood, or jewellery to carry their energy with you.

Spell Enhancements: Incorporate runes into spells by writing them on paper, drawing them on candles (or other objects), or using them in visualizations.

Sigils and Bind Runes: Combine multiple runes to create a sigil or bind rune that embodies a specific intention or protection.

Summary of Different Runes and Their Meanings

Here is a brief overview of some of the key runes from the Elder Futhark and their meanings:

Fehu

Meaning: Wealth, prosperity, abundance

Use Fehu in spells related to attracting financial gain, abundance, and success.

Uruz

Meaning: Strength, vitality, health

Ideal for spells focusing on physical strength, healing, and overcoming challenges.

Thurisaz

Meaning: Protection, defense, conflict

Use Thurisaz for protective spells or to break through obstacles and blockages.

Ansuz

Meaning: Communication, wisdom, divine inspiration

Use: Helpful in spells for enhancing communication, gaining wisdom, and connecting with higher guidance.

Raidho

Meaning: Journey, movement, progress

Use Raidho in spells for safe travel, making progress, or starting change.

Kenaz

Meaning: Knowledge, creativity, revelation

Ideal for spells related to learning, uncovering hidden truths, or enhancing creativity.

Gebo

Meaning: Gift, partnership, generosity

Use Gebo in spells to attract partnerships, strengthen friendships, or enhance generosity.

Wunjo

Meaning: Joy, harmony, success

Perfect for spells aimed at bringing happiness, harmony, and success in various endeavours.

Hagalaz

Meaning: Disruption, transformation, challenges

Use Hagalaz to break old patterns, initiate transformation, or overcome difficulties.

Nauthiz

Meaning: Need, constraint, patience

Use Nauthiz in spells for overcoming obstacles, practicing patience, and finding creative solutions.

Isa

Meaning: Ice, stillness, focus

Ideal for spells requiring concentration, stillness, or cooling down intense emotions.

Jera

Meaning: Harvest, reward, cycles

Use Jera in spells to celebrate achievements, promote growth, and align with natural cycles.

Eihwaz

Meaning: Strength, stability, endurance

Ideal for spells focusing on stability, resilience, and inner strength.

Perthro

Meaning: Mystery, fate, hidden things

Use Perthro in spells to uncover secrets, explore mysteries, or connect with destiny.

Algiz

Meaning: Protection, sanctuary, divine support
  Perfect for protective spells, creating safe spaces, and seeking divine assistance.

Sowilo

Meaning: Sun, success, vitality
  Use Sowilo in spells for success, health, and enhancing personal power.

Tiwaz

Meaning: Justice, honor, leadership
  Use: Ideal for spells related to fairness, achieving goals, and taking leadership roles.

Berkano

Meaning: Growth, fertility, renewal
  Use: Use Berkano in spells for new beginnings, personal growth, and fertility.

Ehwaz

Meaning: Movement, partnership, trust
  Use Ehwaz in spells to enhance trust, strengthen partnerships, and promote smooth transitions.

Mannaz

Meaning: Humanity, self, social order

Ideal for spells related to self-awareness, understanding others, and social harmony.

Laguz

Meaning: Water, intuition, flow

Use Laguz in spells for enhancing intuition, emotional healing, and going with the flow.

Ingwaz

Meaning: Fertility, peace, inner growth

Perfect for spells focusing on personal growth, fertility, and achieving inner peace.

Dagaz

Meaning: Dawn, awakening, transformation

Use Dagaz in spells for new beginnings, enlightenment, and personal transformation.

Othala

Meaning: Heritage, home, inheritance

Ideal for spells related to family, home protection, and connecting with heritage.

Using Runes in Spellcrafting

To incorporate runes into your spellcrafting, consider these steps:

Choose the Appropriate Rune(s): Based on your intention, select the rune that best matches your desired outcome.

Prepare Your Space: Cleanse your space and gather your materials. You may want to have a quiet, focused environment.

Carve or Draw the Rune: You can carve the rune into a candle, draw it on paper, or inscribe it on an object. If you're using a safe alternative to candles, draw the rune on a battery-operated candle or a piece of paper. Other options include painting runes on small river rocks or pebbles with smooth surfaces, painting on glass pebbles, or creating runes from salt dough and baking.

Focus Your Intention: As you work with the rune, focus on your intention. Visualize the rune's energy aligning with your goal.

Activate the Rune: You can activate the rune by saying a chant, lighting a candle, or using visualization techniques. Imagine the rune glowing with energy, bringing your intention to life.

Close Your Spell: Once you feel the spell is complete, thank the runes and any deities or spirits you called upon. Dispose of any materials respectfully, and ground yourself to release excess energy.

Key Takeaway

Runes are a rich and ancient tool for magic and self-discovery. By understanding the meanings of different runes and how to use them, teenage witches can add a unique and powerful element to their practice. Whether used for divination, talismans, or spellcasting, runes offer a connection to ancient wisdom and a pathway to manifesting your intentions. Remember to always approach rune magic with respect and mindfulness, and enjoy the journey of exploring this fascinating form of magical expression.

Chapter 14

TAROT MAGIC AND SPELLCRAFTING

Tarot cards are a versatile and popular tool in modern witchcraft, especially for new witches exploring their magical paths. Beyond their use in divination, tarot cards can enhance spellcrafting, providing symbolism, guidance, and a deeper connection to spiritual energies. This chapter will explore various ways we can incorporate tarot cards into their magical practice, offering practical tips and spell ideas.

Understanding Tarot Cards

A standard tarot deck comprises seventy-eight cards, divided into the Major Arcana (22 cards) and Minor Arcana (56 cards). The Major Arcana cards represent significant life events, spiritual lessons, and overarching themes, while the Minor Arcana cards deal with everyday events and situations. The Minor Arcana is further divided into four suits: Cups, Pentacles, Swords, and Wands, each corresponding to different aspects of life and elements.

Using Tarot Cards in Spellcrafting

Choosing a Card for Your Intention: Select a tarot card representing your spell's intention. For example, the Lovers card can symbolize love and relationships, while the Strength card represents courage and resilience. The Ace of Pentacles is excellent for new beginnings and prosperity spells.

Meditating with Tarot Cards: Use tarot cards as a focus for meditation to gain clarity on your intentions and desires. Sit quietly with the chosen card, contemplating its imagery and symbolism. This can help you connect with the energy you wish to manifest.

Incorporating Cards into Spells: Place the selected card on your altar or within your spell circle. You can enhance its power by surrounding it with corresponding elements, such as crystals, herbs, or other objects that align with your intention. For instance, if you're working on a self-love spell, you might place the Empress card on your altar, surrounded by rose quartz, rose petals, and a mirror.

Creating Tarot Spreads for Spell Work: Design a tarot spread specifically for your spell. This can help you explore different aspects of your intention and how best to manifest it. For example, a three-card spread might include cards for "What I Desire," "What I Need," and "What I Must Do."

Charging and Empowering the Cards: Before using a tarot card in a spell, you can charge it with your energy. Hold the card in your hands, close your eyes, and focus on your intention. Imagine the card glowing with energy that supports your desired outcome.

Using Tarot in Moon Magic: Align your tarot-based spells with the lunar cycle. For example, use the High Priestess card during the New Moon for introspection and setting intentions or the Moon card during the Full Moon for heightened intuition and revelation.

Spell Ideas Incorporating Tarot Cards

Confidence Boost Spell

Card: The Sun

Supplies: Citrine crystal, yellow candle (or a safe alternative), sunflower petals

Instructions: Place The Sun card on your altar with the crystal and petals around it. Visualize yourself radiating confidence and joy. Light the candle and repeat an affirmation like, "I shine with confidence and positivity."

Manifesting Abundance Spell

Card: The Magician
   Supplies: Green candle (or a safe alternative), bay leaves, a coin
   Instructions: Place The Magician card on your altar, with the candle and bay leaves around it. Write your financial goals on the bay leaves. Focus on the card's imagery and visualize abundance flowing into your life. Light the candle and place the coin on the card.

Friendship Harmony Spell

Card: Three of Cups
   Supplies: Blue candle (or a safe alternative), pink roses, a photo of you and your friends
   Instructions: Set up the card and candle with the roses and photo on your altar. Visualize happy and harmonious moments with your friends. Light the candle and say, "May our friendship be joyful and true."

Protection Spell

Card: The Tower (for clearing negative energies)
   Supplies: Black candle (or a safe alternative), obsidian or black tourmaline, salt
   Instructions: Place The Tower card on your altar. Surround it with the crystal and a circle of salt. Visualize the card's energy destroying any negative influences in your life. Light the candle and chant, "I am protected, safe, and secure."

Caring for Your Tarot Cards

Cleansing: Regularly cleanse your cards to keep them energetically clear. You can do this by passing them through incense smoke, placing them under moonlight or sunlight, bathing in fresh rainwater, or using a selenite wand.
   Storage: To protect your tarot cards, store them in a special box, bag, or cloth. This also shows respect for their magical properties. Incorporate the unwrapping into your spell preparation ritual, infusing the cards with more intention.
   Bonding: Spend time with your tarot deck to build a strong connection. Shuffle the cards, draw daily cards for guidance, or use them in meditation.

Alternatives to Tarot Cards

Tarot cards can be purchased, and many of the decks are extremely well-designed. New users could draw and colour their own representation as an alternative to purchasing a full deck. Take inspiration from existing cards but adjust to align with your magic and intention. This is a great opportunity to incorporate a sigil or use colours that match or align with a spell intention.

Do not just duplicate someone else's artwork. Make sure it represents you.

Key Takeaway

Tarot cards are a rich and versatile tool in spellcrafting, offering guidance, insight, and a deeper connection to magical energies. For new witches, incorporating tarot cards into their practice can enhance their understanding of themselves and the world around them. Whether used for divination, meditation, or spellwork, tarot cards can be a valuable ally on your magical journey.

There are similarities between runes and tarot in their divination capabilities, but both can be used as guided reflection. An introductory set of each should provide basic representations of the rune or tarot, including an inverted display. For new users focus on only the standard view to familiarize yourself with the card or stone.

Remember to approach tarot and runes with respect and mindfulness, and enjoy exploring their endless possibilities in your spellcrafting endeavours.

Chapter 15

ASTROLOGY AND SPELLCRAFTING

Astrology, the study of celestial bodies and their influence on human life can be a powerful tool for teenage witches looking to enhance their magical practices. By understanding the basics of astrology, such as zodiac signs, planets, and lunar phases, you can tailor your spells and rituals to align with cosmic energies, amplifying their effectiveness. This chapter will explore how to incorporate astrology into your spellcrafting, including choosing the right astrological timing, using zodiac signs and planets in spells, and creating personalized astrological rituals.

Astrological Basics for Spellcrafting

Zodiac Signs and Their Qualities

The zodiac is divided into 12 signs associated with specific personality traits and energies. The signs are also grouped into four elements: Fire, Earth, Air, and Water.

Signs: Aries, Leo, Sagittarius

Element: Fire

Qualities: Passionate, energetic, bold

Signs: Taurus, Virgo, Capricorn

Element: Earth
  Qualities: Grounded, practical, reliable

Signs: Gemini, Libra, Aquarius

Element: Air
  Qualities: Intellectual, communicative, free-spirited

Signs: Cancer, Scorpio, Pisces

Element: Water
  Qualities: Emotional, intuitive, nurturing

Planets and Their Influences

In astrology, each planet governs specific aspects of life. When a planet is in a particular sign, it influences the energies and themes associated with it.

Planet/Celestial Body:

Sun: Identity, ego, personal power
  Moon: Emotions, intuition, inner life
  Mercury: Communication, intellect, learning
  Venus: Love, beauty, relationships
  Mars: Action, passion, courage
  Jupiter: Expansion, luck, growth
  Saturn: Discipline, responsibility, structure
  Uranus: Innovation, rebellion, change
  Neptune: Dreams, spirituality, illusions
  Pluto: Transformation, power, rebirth

Choosing the Right Astrological Timing

Planetary Days

Each day of the week is associated with a specific planet, which can enhance certain types of spells:

    Monday (Moon): Emotions, intuition, home
    Tuesday (Mars): Courage, action, protection
    Wednesday (Mercury): Communication, learning, travel
    Thursday (Jupiter): Prosperity, growth, success
    Friday (Venus): Love, beauty, relationships
    Saturday (Saturn): Structure, discipline, long-term goals
    Sunday (Sun): Self-expression, creativity, vitality

Time of Day

The time of day can also facilitate or improve different spells.

    Morning: Good for spells that involve new beginnings and fresh energy.
    Afternoon: Ideal for spells related to productivity and growth.
    Evening: A good time for reflection, love, and peace spells.
    Night: Perfect for dream work, introspection, and subconscious connection.

Using Zodiac Signs in Spellcrafting

Personal Spells by Sun Sign: Incorporate your sun sign's qualities into your spells for personal growth. For example, if you're a Leo, focus on spells that boost confidence and creativity.

Compatibility Spells: Use astrology to understand the dynamics between different signs, creating spells that enhance relationships and communication. For instance, a spell to strengthen friendships could focus on harmonizing the elements of the signs involved.

Harnessing Seasonal Energies: Each zodiac season brings unique energies. Tailor your spellcrafting to align with these energies, such as manifesting new opportunities during Aries season (the beginning of the zodiac cycle) or focusing on transformation during Scorpio season.

Creating Astrological Rituals

Lunar Rituals: Create rituals that honour the lunar phases, such as setting intentions during the New Moon and releasing what no longer serves you during the Full Moon.

Solar Returns and Birthdays: Celebrate your solar return (birthday) with a special ritual focusing on your personal goals for the coming year. Reflect on your sun sign's traits and how you can embody them more fully.

Planetary Retrogrades: During planetary retrogrades (when a planet appears to move backward), focus on reflection and reevaluation. For example, revisit old projects during Mercury retrograde and enhance communication clarity.

Sample Spells Using Astrology

New Moon Intention Setting

Purpose: Set new goals and intentions.

Supplies: White or silver paper, pen, moonstone (optional)

Instructions: Write your intentions on the paper, aligning them with the qualities of your sun sign. Hold the paper under the New Moon (or a picture of it), and visualize your goals coming to fruition. Keep the paper in a special place.

Venus Love Charm

Purpose: Open yourself up to the prospect of love.

Supplies: Rose quartz, pink ribbon, rose petals

Instructions: Create a charm on a Friday (Venus's day) by wrapping the rose quartz in the pink ribbon. Place it among the rose petals, and say, "Venus, goddess of love, make me open to accepting love in my life." Carry the charm with you.

Full Moon Release Spell

Purpose: Let go of negative energy and habits.

Supplies: Black candle (optional), paper, pen

Instructions: Write down what you wish to release on the paper. Light the candle (if safe to do so) and focus on the Full Moon's energy. Burn the paper (safely) or tear it up, saying, "Under the Full Moon's light, I release what no longer serves me." Bury the ashes or pieces.

Key Takeaway

Astrology offers a rich and dynamic framework for teenage witches to explore and incorporate into their magical practices. By understanding the influences of the zodiac signs, planets, and lunar phases, you can enhance your spells and rituals, making them more aligned with the cosmic energies at play. Remember, astrology is a tool for self-discovery and empowerment, not a deterministic map of your life. Use it to guide your intentions, understand yourself better, and connect with the universe's rhythms.

Chapter 16

MYSTICAL REFLECTIONS — SCRYING FOR CLARITY AND CALM

In the world of witchcraft, the ancient art of scrying offers a meditative gateway to inner peace and profound insights. Scrying is the practice of gazing into a reflective surface—such as a crystal ball, mirror, or still water—to receive visions and messages. This chapter delves into crystal ball, mirror, and water scrying methods, highlighting how these practices can enhance mental health by promoting self-reflection, mindfulness, and emotional clarity.

The Power of Scrying

Scrying isn't just about foretelling the future; it's a powerful tool for self-discovery and mental well-being. By focusing on a reflective surface, you enter a meditative state that can help ease stress, reduce anxiety, and provide a sense of grounding. The practice encourages you to look inward, confront your subconscious thoughts, and find clarity and answers within yourself.

Preparing Your Sacred Space

Before you begin scrying, creating a conducive environment that fosters tranquility and focus is essential. Here's how to prepare your sacred space:

Choose a Quiet Location: Find a place where you won't be disturbed. Silence is crucial for maintaining focus and entering a meditative state.

Set the Mood: Dim the lights or use candles to create a calm and serene atmosphere. Soft, instrumental music can also be beneficial.

Gather Your Tools: Depending on your preferred method, have your crystal ball, mirror, or bowl of water ready.

Crystal Ball Scrying

A crystal ball is perhaps the most iconic scrying tool. Here's how to use it:

Select Your Crystal Ball: Choose a crystal ball that resonates with you. Clear quartz is popular, but amethyst or rose quartz can also be used.

Sit Comfortably: Sit in a comfortable position with the crystal ball placed on a stand or held in your hands.

Relax and Breathe: Take deep breaths to centre yourself. Focus on your breathing until you feel calm and relaxed.

Gaze into the Ball: Gently gaze into the crystal ball without straining your eyes. Allow your vision to soften and your mind to wander.

Observe and Interpret: Images or symbols may begin to form in the ball. Trust your intuition and interpret the messages you receive. Keep a journal nearby to record your insights.

Mirror Scrying

A mirror can be a powerful portal for scrying. Here's how to practice mirror scrying:

Choose Your Mirror: A black mirror or a regular mirror can be used. Black mirrors are preferred as they reduce distractions.

Position the Mirror: Place the mirror at eye level and ensure it's clean and free of smudges.

Dim the Lights: Use candles to softly illuminate the room, ensuring that the light is not reflecting directly in the mirror.

Focus and Relax: Sit comfortably and focus on your reflection or the darkness of the mirror. Allow your mind to quiet and your thoughts to slow.

Watch for Visions: As you gaze, you may see shapes, images, or even scenes forming. Trust your inner voice to guide the interpretation of these visions.

Water Scrying

Water scrying is a gentle and accessible method that uses the reflective surface of water. Here's how to do it:

Prepare Your Bowl: Use a dark, shallow bowl filled with water. Adding herbs like lavender or rosemary can enhance the experience.

Set the Scene: Place the bowl on a flat surface, and position a candle to reflect light onto the water.

Calm Your Mind: Take a few moments to breathe deeply and relax your body.

Gaze into the Water: Look into the water's surface, allowing your eyes to soften. Be open to what you might see.

Interpret the Ripples: Pay attention to any images, patterns, or feelings that arise. Water can be effective in revealing emotional truths.

Integrating Scrying into Your Daily Routine

Scrying can be a regular practice to maintain mental health and emotional balance. Here are some tips to integrate it into your daily life:

Set Intentions: Begin each scrying session with a clear intention. Whether seeking guidance, clarity, or calm, setting an intention helps focus your session.

Practice Regularly: Make scrying a part of your weekly routine. Consistent practice enhances your ability to receive and interpret visions.

Keep a Journal: Document your experiences and insights in a journal. Over time, you may notice patterns or recurring themes that provide a deeper understanding.

Combine with Other Practices: Scrying pairs well with other mindful practices like meditation, yoga, or journaling.

Develop Patience: Often, our mind will become distracted before we are relaxed enough to experience a vision. That is okay. It can take a long time to develop the skills to remain fixed on the scrying object while softening your gaze and relaxing into the experience. To maintain focus, reflecting on how the breath feels and moving in and out of your body may be helpful. Focusing our mind on the breath can minimize mental distractions like "What will I eat for lunch tomorrow?" However, if your mind wanders, that is okay. Just make note of it and try to bring your attention back to scrying.

Key Takeaway

Scrying is a sacred practice that offers a unique way to connect with your inner self and the universe. Through the reflective surfaces of crystal balls, mirrors, and water, you can achieve a state of mindfulness that promotes mental health and emotional clarity. Embrace these ancient techniques to navigate the complexities of teenage life with wisdom, peace, and confidence.

Chapter 17

THE POWER OF ANIMAL REPRESENTATION IN WITCHCRAFT

In many spiritual and magical traditions, animals are seen as powerful symbols that embody certain qualities, energies, and wisdom. Known as animal totems, spirit animals, or familiars, these representations can be incorporated into witchcraft to enhance spells, rituals, and personal growth. By connecting with the energy of a particular animal, witches can draw on its traits and strengths, using them to support their intentions and magical workings.

In addition, if you recognize that you gravitate to a particular animal, perhaps a favourite, consider what that animal totem signifies in you. I have loved animals of all kinds throughout my life. My dreams have featured numerous bears and very large fish or whales. However, consistently, over the last twenty years, I have felt drawn to rhinoceroses. There is something about them that brings me joy. In case you are wondering or share the same affinity, rhinos represent resilience, emotional strength, and the wisdom to navigate life's trials. These also happen to be a passion for me.

How to Incorporate Animal Representation

There are several ways to incorporate animal representations into your magical practices:

Symbols and Statues: Invoke animals' energy by placing statues, figurines, or drawings on your altar or in your sacred space.

Animal Imagery in Tools: Decorate your magical tools, such as wands, chalices, or pentacles, with images or symbols of animals that resonate with your intentions.

Meditation and Visualization: Meditate on a specific animal's energy, visualizing its presence and connecting with its qualities. You can also use guided meditations to meet and communicate with your spirit animal.

Animal Correspondences in Spells: Incorporate animal imagery or symbolism in spell work. For example, using a feather for a bird, a shell for a sea creature, or an animal's footprint in a drawing.

Dream Work: Keep a dream journal and pay attention to animals that appear in your dreams. These can offer insights into your subconscious mind and guide you in your magical practices.

Nature Walks and Observations: Spend time in nature observing animals. Note their behavior, characteristics, and how they make you feel. This can deepen your connection to the animal world and provide inspiration for your magical practices.

Common Animals in Witchcraft and Their Significance

Cat

Symbolism: Independence, mystery, intuition.

Uses: Cats are often associated with witches and are believed to enhance psychic abilities. They can be called upon for protection and insight.

Owl

Symbolism: Wisdom, knowledge, secrets.

Uses: The owl's association with the night and the moon makes it a powerful symbol for uncovering hidden truths and enhancing wisdom.

Wolf

Symbolism: Loyalty, instinct, strength.

Uses: Wolves represent strong family ties and community. They can be invoked for guidance, protection, and finding one's true path.

Raven

Symbolism: Transformation, magic, communication.

Uses: Ravens are messengers between worlds and are often associated with magical transformation and change. They are used in spells to communicate and connect with the spiritual realm.

Deer

Symbolism: Gentleness, intuition, new beginnings.

Uses: Deer symbolize peace and gentleness. They can be called upon for guidance during new beginnings and to enhance one's intuition.

Snake

Symbolism: Rebirth, healing, transformation.

Uses: Snakes shed their skin, making them powerful symbols of renewal and healing. They are used in spells for transformation and overcoming obstacles.

Bear

Symbolism: Strength, courage, grounding.

Uses: Bears are symbols of strength and grounding. They can be invoked for protection, courage, and inner strength.

Butterfly

Symbolism: Transformation, beauty, change.

Uses: Butterflies represent personal growth and transformation. They are used in spells to bring about change and embrace new phases of life.

Horse

Symbolism: Freedom, power, travel.

Uses: Horses are symbols of freedom and power. They can be used in spells to enhance personal freedom, strength, and movement forward.

Fox

Symbolism: Cleverness, adaptability, stealth.

Uses: Foxes are associated with cunning and adaptability. They can also solve problems and navigate tricky situations.

Dolphin

Symbolism: Playfulness, communication, harmony.

Uses: Dolphins are symbols of joy and communication. They are used in spells to enhance communication, joy, and harmony in relationships.

Lion

Symbolism: Courage, leadership, strength.

Uses: Lions represent courage and leadership. They can be invoked for strength and confidence in leadership roles or challenging situations.

Hawk

Symbolism: Vision, focus, clarity.

Uses: Hawks are symbols of keen vision and insight. They are used in spells to enhance focus and gain clarity in decision-making.

Rabbit

Symbolism: Fertility, abundance, agility.

Uses: Rabbits are associated with fertility and abundance. They can be called upon in spells for prosperity and swift action.

Turtle

Symbolism: Longevity, patience, stability.

Uses: Turtles symbolize patience and stability. They are used in spells for grounding and long-term success.

Eagle

Symbolism: Freedom, perspective, power.

Uses: Eagles are symbols of freedom and higher perspective. They can be invoked to gain a broader view of a situation and for personal empowerment.

Spider

Symbolism: Creativity, connection, weaving fate.

Uses: Spiders are symbols of creativity and the interconnectedness of life. They are used in spells for creativity and weaving one's destiny.

Frog

Symbolism: Transformation, cleansing, fertility.

Uses: Frogs symbolize transformation and cleansing. They are used in spells for healing and fertility.

Elephant

Symbolism: Wisdom, memory, strength.

Uses: Elephants are symbols of wisdom and strength. They can be called upon for patience, memory, and overcoming obstacles.

Crow

Symbolism: Magic, mystery, intelligence.

Uses: Crows are associated with magic and mystery. As a highly intelligent species, they can be used in spells to gain knowledge and access hidden wisdom.

Dog

Symbolism: Loyalty, protection, intuition

Uses: When working with dog symbolism, practitioners can draw upon these qualities to enhance spells and rituals, particularly those related to protection, friendship, loyalty, and strengthening bonds with loved ones.

Whales

Symbolism: Wisdom/ancient knowledge, amplification, intuition

Uses: Whales represent a greater depth of knowledge. Practitioners could incorporate whale imagery into complex spells.

Rhinoceros

Symbolism: Resilience, emotional strength, wisdom to navigate life's trials

Uses: Draw on the rhinoceros in times of emotional pain or when feeling overwhelmed. Practitioners could charge a symbolic representation to carry with them as a charm.

Ethical Considerations and Respect for Animals

When incorporating animal symbolism into your magical practices, it's essential to approach it with respect and reverence. Avoid using real animal parts, as this can be unethical and disrespectful. Instead, use representations like statues, images, and symbols. Always research the cultural significance of animals and ensure that you are not appropriating or misrepresenting traditions that are not your own. You create a respectful and powerful connection in your magical practice by honoring the spirit and energy of the animals you work with.

Animal representations can offer deep insights and powerful energies for your magical workings. By understanding and connecting with these symbols, you can enhance your spells, rituals, and personal growth in meaningful ways.

Chapter 18

OTHER MAGICAL ELEMENTS TO INCORPORATE INTO SPELLCRAFTING

Many everyday actions could be incorporated into rituals and spells. Even deciding which shoe to put on first could be a mindful activity intended to start a journey on the right foot. You are empowered to determine what might become part of your rituals.

Incorporating simple, everyday actions with a magical intention can be a wonderful way to infuse daily life with mindfulness, grounding, and a sense of connection to one's spiritual practice. Here are some easy and meaningful practices that can serve both as a form of magical work and as tools for mental well-being:

Spoon Stirring Direction:

In various magical and spiritual traditions, the direction in which you stir or turn a spoon during rituals or spellcasting can carry specific symbolic significance. This belief stems from the broader concept that certain directions hold unique energies or meanings. Here's a breakdown of how the direction can be interpreted:

Clockwise (Deosil)

In many traditions, stirring or moving clockwise is drawing in positive energy, blessings, and growth. It is often associated with invoking, increasing, or attracting things. For example, stirring clockwise might be used when you want to bring good fortune, love, health, or prosperity into your life. This direction is considered to align with the movement of the sun, which is seen as a symbol of light, life, and positive energy.

Counterclockwise (Widdershins)

Conversely, stirring counterclockwise is typically associated with banishing, decreasing, or removing. It is often used in rituals aimed at clearing away negative energy, breaking curses, or letting go of unwanted habits or influences. This direction is thought to represent a reversal or undoing, working against the natural flow to dispel or cleanse.

Incorporating this concept into everyday practices or spellcraft can be simple yet meaningful. For example, if someone is making an herbal tea to attract love or positivity, they might stir the tea clockwise, focusing on the positive qualities they wish to draw into their life. Conversely, if they prepare a cleansing bath or potion to rid themselves of stress or negativity, they might stir counterclockwise, visualizing the release and removal of those unwanted energies.

While the magical significance of stirring direction is a tradition found in various cultures and practices, it's essential to remember that intention is a critical component in any magical work. The direction of stirring can enhance the focus and symbolism of a spell or ritual, but the practitioner's mindset and purpose truly give the action its power.

Magical Rituals and Mental Health Well-Being

Breathing with Intention

Magical Infusion: Use deep breathing exercises to set intentions. Inhale deeply, drawing in energy or positive qualities like calm, focus, or confidence. Exhale, releasing stress, negativity, or other unwanted emotions.

Mental Well-being: This practice can reduce stress, improve focus, and promote relaxation.

Washing Hands or Face

Magical Infusion: While washing hands or face, visualize cleansing away negativity or impurities. You can also set an intention to wash away the day's stresses or to prepare for a fresh start.

    Mental Well-being: This ritual can serve as a moment of mindfulness, helping to reset and refresh your mindset.

Walking with Purpose

Magical Infusion: Consciously connect with the earth beneath your feet during a walk. With each step, imagine drawing strength and grounding energy from the earth or releasing stress and negativity into it.

    Mental Well-being: Walking is a great way to clear the mind, reduce anxiety, and gain clarity.

Eating Mindfully

Magical Infusion: Before eating, express gratitude for the food and its sources. With each bite, you can also set an intention for nourishment, healing, or energy.

    Mental Well-being: Mindful eating promotes a healthy relationship with food and can enhance the experience of taste and nourishment.

Brushing Hair

Magical Infusion: As you brush your hair, visualize removing any mental clutter or negative thoughts. Alternatively, you can imagine strengthening your inner and outer self with each stroke.

    Mental Well-being: This can be a soothing ritual that promotes self-care and relaxation.

Making Your Bed

Magical Infusion: While making your bed, set an intention for a peaceful and restful night. You can also imbue the action with a sense of order and clarity for the day ahead.

Mental Well-being: A tidy bed can provide a sense of accomplishment and a calm start to the day.

Sipping Tea or Coffee

Magical Infusion: As you prepare and drink your tea or coffee, focus on the warmth and comfort it brings. Depending on the blend, set an intention for energy, relaxation, or focus.

Mental Well-being: This practice can be a comforting ritual that provides a moment of peace and mindfulness.

Journaling or Writing

Magical Infusion: Journaling can be a way to set intentions, reflect on experiences, or manifest desires. You can also write affirmations or release worries and negative thoughts.

Mental Well-being: Journaling can clarify thoughts, release emotions, and serve as a creative outlet.

Tidying Up

Magical Infusion: While tidying a space, visualize clearing away stagnant energy and making room for positive, fresh energy. You can also set an intention for clarity and organization in your thoughts and life.

Mental Well-being: A clean space can reduce stress and create a more comfortable living environment.

Stretching or Yoga

Magical Infusion: During stretching or yoga, focus on releasing tension and opening yourself up to new possibilities. You can also set an intention for physical and emotional flexibility.

Mental Well-being: Physical movement helps release stress and improve mental clarity.

Watering Plants

Magical Infusion: As you water your plants, think about nurturing and growth, not just for the plants, but also for yourself. Set an intention for personal development or healing.

Mental Well-being: Caring for plants can be a calming and grounding experience, promoting a connection to nature.

Incorporating these practices into daily life can turn ordinary moments into mindfulness and intentional living opportunities. By aligning these actions with personal goals and spiritual beliefs, teenagers can create a daily practice that supports their mental well-being and spiritual growth.

Chapter 19

SPELLCRAFTING AND SPELLCASTING

Spellcrafting

Now that you have all this knowledge of different elements of magic and even a few spell examples, it is time to combine all this knowledge and start building your own spells. While this book has provided some spells, you are not limited to these spells or even the directions provided. There are some books or characterizations of witchcraft being labour-intensive or overcomplicated. It shouldn't, though. Creating and casting a spell that aligns with your intent and ideology should feel easy and almost liberating.

Begin with Intention: Magic is about intention. Before you craft a spell or ritual, meditate on the intention of the spell. Does it align with do no harm?

What Type of Magic: Determine what type of magic you want to perform. Are you starting a spell to create a talisman or magic bag to carry with you? Are you wanting to perform a ritual-type spell? Perhaps something meditative?

Supplies and Symbols: While supplies and symbols are unnecessary, they help focus the intention and energy of the spell. Consider what materials would complement the spell. Be prescriptive and only use the supplies that you feel resonate with the spell.

Determine Day and Time: Using all the elements reviewed, determine the day and time to complete your spell.

Create Your Spell: Like a dinner recipe, creating a spell benefits from instructions. Use a journal or create your own Magic Tome or Book of Shadows that includes all the materials, steps, location, and day/time to cast the spell.

Spellcasting

Spellcasting is a beautiful and empowering practice that allows you to focus on your intentions and harness the energies of the universe to bring about positive change. For teenagers, spellcasting can be a creative and insightful way to explore your desires, set goals, and enhance your personal growth. In this chapter, we'll guide you through the basics of organizing your supplies, choosing the right timing for your spells, and crafting your own magical intentions.

Organizing Your Supplies

Before casting a spell, gathering and organizing your supplies is essential. This prepares you practically and helps set the mood for your ritual.

Sacred Space: Create a quiet, personal space where you feel comfortable and undisturbed. This could be a corner of your room, a small altar, or a cozy nook.

Tools and Ingredients: Common items include candles, crystals, herbs, oils, incense, and a journal for writing spells and reflections. Keep your supplies in a designated box or drawer, and treat them with respect.

Altar: An altar is a focal point for your magical work. It can be as simple as a small table with meaningful items like candles, crystals, a bowl of water, and representations of the elements. Arrange these items in a way that feels right to you.

Journal, Tome, Book of Shadows, or Grimoire: Keep a journal to record your spells, intentions, and experiences. This personal record, often called a Book of Shadows, helps track your progress and learn from each experience.

Reflect and Revise

After you complete your spell or ritual, reflect on what felt right and what should change for future casting. Keep track of how you feel before, during, and after the casting.

You can add your thoughts and experiences directly to your journal, tome, or Book of Shadows. Like perfecting a recipe, you may keep work-in-progress spells in a different journal from your official Magical Tome, Book of Shadows, or Grimoire.

Chapter 20

SPELLS

hese spells are designed to be safe and accessible, emphasizing mindfulness, intention, and the use of everyday objects. Remember, the most essential element in any spell is your focused intention and belief in the magic you are creating. Always approach spellcasting with respect and a positive mindset.

These spells can be modified to suit your needs, supplies, and comfort level.

Self-Confidence Charm

This is a perfect charm to add a little confidence on a challenging day. It is suggested that you complete the charm on a Sunday as a preparation for the following week, but the spell can be done or repeated on any day.

Supplies
- Yellow candle or alternative

- Yellow or gold crystal (ex: citrine)

- Paper and pen or marker

Instructions
- On a Sunday morning, light the yellow candle and hold the citrine in your hand.

- Write an affirmation like "I am confident and capable."

- Fold the paper and place it under the candle.

- Visualize yourself radiating confidence. Extinguish the candle.

- Carry the citrine with you as a charm.

Friendship Blessing

Supplies
- Pink candle or alternative

- Rose quartz

- Lavender essential oil or alternative

Instructions
- On a Friday evening, light the pink candle.

- Anoint the candle with a few drops of lavender oil or place the lavender alternative at the base of the candle.

- Hold the rose quartz and think of the friendships you want to nurture.

- Say, "I attract loving and supportive friends."

- Let the candle burn out safely, or extinguish it after a few minutes of concentration.

Study and Focus Spell

Supplies
- Blue cloth

- A small piece of lapis lazuli or alternative crystal

- Rosemary.

Instructions

- On an afternoon, place the rosemary and lapis lazuli on the blue cloth and tie the bundle.

- Focus on your study goals and say, "My mind is sharp, and I am focused."

- Keep the bundle with you while you study.

- Repeat the ritual daily to recharge the bundle.

Dream Clarity Ritual

Supplies

- Rune Perthro or Kenaz or representation

- Amethyst crystal or alternative

- Cloth bag or sachet

- A dream journal and writing tool

Instructions

- In the evening, before bed, place the rune(s) and amethyst in the bag.

- Leave your journal and writing tool next to your bed

- Holding the bag/sachet repeat "I remember and understand my dreams" five times with intention.

- Place the bag/sachet under your pillow.

- Lie down to sleep and repeat the mantra again five more times.

- In the morning or when you awake, write your dreams in the journal.

Protection Bubble

Supplies

- A black crystal or mineral or representation (tourmaline, onyx, hematite, smoky quartz)

- A small bowl of salt

- A pinch of grated clove.

- A small spoon or chopstick depending on the size of the bowl

Instructions

- Add the grated clove to the salt.

- Use a spoon or chopstick to mix the salt and clove, turning twice clockwise and counterclockwise. This will visually push away negativity and destructive energy and attract positive and protective energy.

- Hold the black crystal and imagine a protective bubble around you.

- Sprinkle salt in a circle around your sacred space.

- Say, "I am protected."

- Carry the black crystal for ongoing protection.

Affirmation Jar Spell

Supplies

- Small jar

- Paper and pen or marker

- small crystal(s), herbs, or other magical element(s).

Instructions

- Write positive affirmations or desires on the slips of paper.

- Place them in the jar along with the appropriate magical element(s).

- Seal the jar and gently shake it, visualizing your affirmations coming to life.

Crystal Grid for Focus

Supplies

- Crystals (such as clear quartz, amethyst, fluorite)

- Paper and pen or marker

- Optional – sacred geometry grid of your choice.

Instructions

- Arrange the crystals in a grid pattern on the paper.

- In the centre, write your intention for focus and clarity.

- Leave the grid undisturbed in a quiet place to amplify your focus.

Flower Blessing

Supplies

- Fresh flowers or representation

- Water in a bowl or jar

Instructions

- Fill a bowl with water and place the fresh flowers in it.

- Speak your intention over the water, then use it to bless yourself by dipping your fingers and anointing your forehead or hands.

This spell also works beautifully with watercolour paintings of flowers. The image dissolves in the water, infusing it with the flower energy you created in the painting.

Herbal Sachet for Peace

Supplies

- Small fabric pouch

- Calming herbs (such as lavender and chamomile)

- Ribbon (yellow, white, or pink).

Instructions

- Fill the pouch with the herbs.

- Tie it closed with the ribbon while stating your intention for peace.

- Keep the sachet under your pillow or in your room.

Sound Cleansing

Supplies

- Singing bowl, bell, or chimes. Sound applications or videos could also be used but less interactive.

Instructions

- Gently play the singing bowl, bell, or chimes to cleanse your space and yourself.

- As the sound resonates, focus on releasing negativity and inviting positive energy.

Nature Connection Spell

Supplies

- A natural object (stone, leaf, feather)

- Journal, and pen.

Instructions

- Find a natural object that resonates with you.

- Hold it and meditate on your intention.

- Write your reflections in a journal, focusing on the energy of the object and how it connects to your goal.

Mirror Manifestation

Supplies

- Mirror

- Dry-erase marker or lipstick.

Instructions

- Write your intention or affirmation on the mirror with the marker or lipstick.

- Each time you see it, speak the words aloud and visualize them coming true.

Ribbon Wish

Supplies

- Ribbon or string (colour paired with the intent)

- Tree branch or small plant.

Instructions

- Write your wish or intention on the ribbon.

- Focus on your desire and tie it to a tree branch or plant.

- Leave it there as a symbol of your intention growing and manifesting.

Water Scrying

Supplies

- Bowl of water

- Quiet, dimly lit space.

- Optional – runes, crystals, herbs/flowers

Instructions

- Gaze into the bowl of water, allowing your mind to relax.

- Focus on a question or intention and observe any images or feelings that arise from the water's reflection.

Consider adding runes, crystals, or herbs/flowers to the water to generate more ripples and characteristics on the water's surface.

Plant Spell for Growth

Supplies

- Potted plant

- Small piece of paper and pen

- Soil if required.

Instructions

- Write your intention for personal growth on the paper.

- Bury it in the soil of the potted plant.

- Care for the plant as a symbol of nurturing your growth.

Consider including an affirmation each time your water the plant that ties with the intent of the note.

Symbol Drawing

Supplies
- Paper, coloured pencils, or markers.

Instructions
- Draw a symbol that represents your intention or desire.

- Colour it in with intention, focusing on the energy you wish to manifest.

- Keep the drawing somewhere visible.

Wind Chime Wish

Supplies
- Wind chimes and a place to hang them.

Instructions
- As you hang the wind chimes, speak your intention or wish.

- Each time the chimes ring, imagine your wish being carried by the wind.

Sun and Moon Meditation

Supplies
- A sunny or moonlit space.

Instructions
- Find a comfortable spot where you can bask in the sunlight or moonlight.

- Close your eyes and meditate, absorbing the energy and focusing on your intention.

Salt Circle Protection

Supplies

- Salt

Instructions

- Sprinkle a circle of salt around your space or yourself while focusing on protection.

- Visualize a shield forming around you, keeping negativity at bay.

Feather Wish

Supplies

- Feather

- Paper and pen or marker

Instructions

- Write your wish on the paper.

- Wrap it around the feather and place it in a safe place.

- Each time you see the feather, focus on your wish coming true.

Crystal Charging

Supplies

- Crystal

- Sunny or moonlit spot.

Instructions

- Place your crystal in a sunny or moonlit spot to charge.

- As it absorbs the energy, hold the crystal and set your intention.

- Leave the crystal to bathe in the energy.

Nature Walk Grounding

Supplies

- Comfortable shoes

- Natural setting.

Instructions

- Take a walk in nature, focusing on the sights, sounds, and smells around you.

- As you walk, ground yourself by imagining roots growing from your feet into the earth.

Stone Gratitude

Supplies

- Small stones

- A jar

- Optional – paint or markers

Instructions

- Each day, find a small stone and hold it, thinking of something you're grateful for.

- Place the stone in the jar as a physical representation of your gratitude.

- You can add additional depth by marking each stone.

- You could choose to mark it with a representative colour, a word, a rune, or any combination.

These stones would be used in future spell creation as objects infused with gratitude.

Letting Go of Unwanted Thoughts

Supplies
- Paper and pen

- Paints

Instructions
- Lightly write down the unwanted thought on a piece of paper

- Recognize that it is just a thought, not an action

- Paint over the unwanted thought, visualizing replacing it with the positive energy represented by the coloured paints

Unwanted or intrusive thoughts can occur at any time and are not necessarily bad. They can represent anxiety or simply a random thought that has gotten stuck. Try to avoid judging your unwanted thoughts. If it offers no value, let it go.

Key Takeaway

Spellcasting is a journey of self-discovery and empowerment. As a new witch, this practice can help you navigate the challenges of growing up with clarity, confidence, and a sense of purpose. Remember to always respect your own boundaries and the surrounding energies. The most powerful spells come from a place of positive intention and a genuine desire for growth. Enjoy exploring your magical path, and trust in your unique power to create the changes you seek.

Chapter 21

INTEGRATING MODERN WITCHCRAFT WITH DAILY LIFE

As we conclude our journey through modern witchcraft, it's time to explore how you can seamlessly integrate these practices into your everyday life. Whether you're a student balancing school, social life, and other responsibilities, or simply someone seeking a deeper connection to your spiritual self, incorporating witchcraft into your daily routine can enrich your life in meaningful ways. This final chapter offers practical tips for making witchcraft a natural part of your daily life, balancing it with other responsibilities, and reflecting on personal growth and self-awareness.

Practical Tips for Daily Witchcraft Practices

Morning Rituals: Start your day with a simple ritual to set a positive tone. This could be lighting a candle, pulling a tarot card for daily guidance, or setting an intention. Morning rituals can help ground you and prepare you for the day ahead.

Mindful Breathing and Meditation: Take a few minutes each day to practice mindful breathing or meditation. This can be a time to centre yourself, clear your mind, and connect with your inner self. Use this quiet time to reflect on your intentions and goals.

Daily Affirmations: Create a list of affirmations that resonate with you. These can be statements like "I am confident and capable" or "I attract positive energy into my life." Repeating these affirmations can boost your confidence and reinforce your intentions.

Nature Walks and Grounding: Spend time in nature whenever possible. Whether it's a walk in the park, a hike, or simply sitting outside, connecting with nature can be a powerful way to ground yourself and recharge your energy.

Moon Phases and Rituals: Pay attention to the moon phases and consider incorporating them into your practice. For example, use the new moon for setting intentions and the full moon for releasing what no longer serves you. These lunar rituals can help you align with the natural cycles of the universe.

Journaling: Keep a journal to document your thoughts, experiences, and spiritual growth. Writing about your daily experiences, dreams, and feelings can help you process emotions and track your progress over time.

Creating Sacred Space: Designate a small area in your room as a sacred space. This can be a place where you meditate, perform rituals, or simply sit and reflect. Decorate it with meaningful objects, such as crystals, candles, and personal symbols.

Incorporating Spells into Daily Tasks: Make everyday tasks magical by incorporating simple spells or affirmations. For example, stir your morning tea or coffee clockwise while thinking of positive intentions, or visualize protection while putting on jewelry.

Using Crystals and Talismans: Carry crystals or talismans that resonate with your intentions. For example, amethyst for calmness, rose quartz for love, or tiger's eye for confidence. These can serve as physical reminders of your intentions throughout the day.

Balancing Witchcraft with School, Social Life, and Other Responsibilities

Balancing spiritual practices with school, social life, and other responsibilities can be challenging as a teenager. Here are some tips to help you find that balance:

Prioritize and Plan: Set aside specific times for your spiritual practices. This might be in the morning, before bed, or during breaks. Having a consistent schedule can help you maintain your practices without feeling overwhelmed.

Be Flexible: Life can be unpredictable, and it's okay if you can't stick to your spiritual routine every day. Be flexible and adjust your practices as needed. Remember, even small moments of mindfulness can be powerful.

Integrate Practices into Existing Routines: Find ways to incorporate witchcraft into your existing routines. For example, if you're studying, you can use crystals to enhance focus, or if you're spending time with friends, you can share positive affirmations or practice mindfulness together.

Self-Care and Boundaries: Make self-care a priority. Taking care of yourself physically, emotionally, and spiritually is important. Set boundaries to protect your energy and avoid overcommitting.

Community Support: Engage with like-minded individuals who understand your spiritual journey. This can be through local groups, online communities, or close friends. Having a supportive network can help you stay grounded and motivated.

Reflecting on Personal Growth and Self-Awareness

As you integrate witchcraft into your daily life, take time to reflect on your personal growth and self-awareness. Here are some prompts and practices to help you with this reflection:

Daily Reflection: At the end of each day, take a few moments to reflect on what you've learned, how you've felt, and any spiritual insights you've gained. This can be done through journaling or quiet contemplation.

Monthly Review: Each month, review your journal entries, notes, and any rituals you've performed. Reflect on the patterns you've noticed, the progress you've made, and areas you'd like to explore further.

Setting New Intentions: As you grow and evolve, your goals and intentions may change. Regularly reassess your intentions and set new ones that align with your current path.

Celebrate Milestones: Celebrate your achievements and milestones, both big and small. Whether it's mastering a new skill, overcoming a challenge, or simply maintaining a daily practice, acknowledge and honor your progress.

Embrace Change: Understand that personal growth is a continuous journey. Embrace the changes you experience and be open to new perspectives and practices. Growth often comes from stepping out of your comfort zone and exploring new areas of your spirituality.

Conclusion

Integrating modern witchcraft into your daily life is a beautiful way to connect with your inner self, enhance your well-being, and navigate the challenges of adolescence. You can create a fulfilling and empowered life by incorporating simple rituals and practices, balancing them with other responsibilities, and reflecting on your personal growth.

Remember, witchcraft is a deeply personal and unique journey. There is no one-size-fits-all approach, and your practice may evolve over time. Trust your intuition, follow your interests, and enjoy the journey. As you continue to explore the magical world of modern witchcraft, may you find joy, peace, and a deeper understanding of yourself and the world around you. Blessed be!

Thank you

T hank you for purchasing this book and support.

If you enjoyed this book, please consider providing a review on Amazon. If you have feedback or suggestions for future enhancements, please email me directly at Kelsey.Pearce.Grit@gmail.com

I have created a spell crafting workbook with colour resources for intention elements along with eighty templates to create your own spells, charms, and rituals. This resource is available at Amazon. ISBN 978-1-7382905-6-7